ALSO HERE

ALSO HERE

LOVE, LITERACY, AND THE LEGACY OF THE
HOLOCAUST

BROOKE RANDEL

TORTOISE BOOKS
CHICAGO

"Painfully aware of my limitations, I watched helplessly as language became an obstacle. It became clear that it would be necessary to invent a new language."

— Elie Wiesel

PROLOGUE

The story goes like this: I was born in a car. It was a hot summer night and my parents were scrambling to leave the house. My mom's water had broken and the contractions were kicking in. They buckled my brother Scott, then four years old and up way past his bedtime, into his car seat. They needed someone to watch him while they were at the hospital. My parents jumped in the car—a brown station wagon, bought only a week earlier—and sped to Bubbie's house, a forty-five minute drive away.

As my family pulled up to the small brick house, Bubbie opened the door and ushered them all inside. They'd barely arrived when my mom's contractions intensified, surging in frequency. She called her doctor to ask what they should do and got an answering service instead. Not that there was anything the doctor could say or do. The delivery was happening here and it was happening now.

Somehow, my mom still thought they might make it to the hospital. She waddled back to the car and everyone else followed. No one knew what time it was except that it was late. My mom stepped into the backseat, breathing in and out like an accordion. Frozen in the front yard, my dad held Scott in his arms and they watched, either in awe, astonishment, or complete and total fear. Only Bubbie thought to get a towel. She ran back into the house, but couldn't find one in all the rush. She grabbed a large white tablecloth and bolted to the car. The scene was so fast and frantic, my mom didn't have time to take off her maternity shorts. No matter. This was it. My mom pushed and there I was, born into my grandma's hands.

While my parents debated whether or not to call an ambulance—they ended up doing so, and the whole block woke to strobing red lights, wondering what in the world was going on—Bubbie wrapped me in the tablecloth she'd found inside. She bundled me tightly and cradled me in the nook of her arm, keeping my tiny body warm. Like that, she became my makeshift incubator until a real one could arrive. She looked down at me with big eyes, pulled me in close. In that darkened driveway, on that hot June night when nothing went as planned, Bubbie held me in a tablecloth and introduced me to the world.

This is not my memory. It belongs to her. She's offered it to me throughout my life, on birthdays and visits, and over the phone. I've collected pieces from my mom and dad, from old home videos. It's Scott's first memory, an alarming scene made all the more so by the wolf stories Bubbie told him after everyone else left for the hospital. Her stories always featured the same character, a grandma named Bubbie Beitzah who saved the day in scary situations. I grew up listening to these stories, too. Once, Bubbie Beitzah saved her little ones from a wolf by sewing a boulder into its stomach while it slept. Another time she set a trap for a bear inside her house while her grandkids watched from the safety of her skirt. I never knew where these stories came from— certainly not from any book—but I loved hearing them. They felt strange but comforting, familiar and fantastic all at once. Who was this woman? What was this world? I knew nothing but wonder, my mouth ajar as Bubbie unwrapped details like a roll of tape.

This is not my memory, but it is my story. I've shaped it with paragraphs and punctuation, put in structure where there was none. At no point did I want to insert myself, but there I am in the syntax and spaces, gathered lines and empty gullies. That longing, that's mine. That voice, those doubts, the very many mistakes. It takes a lot of grappling to get a memory to sit still. They can be amorphous on their own, all-consuming. At other times, they're quiet and elusory, evasive even. Sometimes I think about memory, but describe my grandma.

By the end of the Holocaust, Bubbie had nothing but her memories. She placed them in her hands and crossed a continent twice, an ocean once. There was never anything else to hold. In late 2015, she placed her memories in my hands one by one, let me do with them as I pleased. She said, "Alone is lonely." She said, "You know." There were many times I did not know, and just enough that I did.

For a week after my birth, Bubbie cleaned the family car. She flushed it with water, scrubbed out the stains. Her hands worked in circles, up, down and around. May this ugly brown car be clean. May it smell like lemons. May it drive us forward, take us somewhere new, bring us back again. As the story goes, she cleaned it very well.

ONE

I had fifteen minutes. I slipped out of my work clothes and into a t-shirt and tights. I was meeting friends at the climbing gym and did not want to miss my train. In the kitchen, I filled a pot with water, opened a pack of ravioli, and called my grandma.

"I have an umbrella for you," she said once I told her who it was, though I don't think that mattered.

"I don't need an umbrella," I said.

"What?"

I shouted into my phone. "I'm good. I don't need an umbrella!"

Golda Indig, or Bubbie as I call her, was in her mid-eighties and living on her own in a condo in south Florida. I was a few years out of college and sharing an apartment with my best friend in Philadelphia. Bubbie and I hadn't lived in the same state since I was three, so I was used to calling her on the phone every other week. Despite my post-work rush, I knew I had plenty of time—our phone calls rarely lasted more than four minutes and often less than two.

"You should write about my life," she said. "What happened in the war."

I was thrown by this transition, made so swiftly it was almost as if the topics were related. Free umbrella, life story. I didn't know what she was talking about.

"Um. OK, Bubbie. Maybe."

As I got the stovetop going, our conversation fell into its usual patter. She asked me how my brother Scott was doing and I told her: he's good. I asked her about the weather down in Florida and she told me: it's hot. We talked because we liked hearing one another's voice, not because we ever had much to say. After a minute or two, we both said goodbye and I love you and kissed our phones.

By the time my food was ready, I wasn't thinking about Bubbie's suggestion for me to write her story. I had other things on my mind, namely my latest climbing injury, a torn tendon in my left ring finger. Any traces of our conversation—her life, the umbrella, my brother—dissipated as I finished eating dinner, taped up my finger and booked it for the train.

A week or two later, I called Bubbie again, this time as I was leaving work. I worked for a small ad agency as a copywriter. It was my job to turn convoluted matters into simple, clever lines, campaigns with legs. I wrote billboards and banner ads, radio spots, TV scripts, everything short and snappy. I liked the rhythm of the work, the ease and clarity it required.

"How are you doing, Bubbie? How's your knee?" I asked outside the office.

"I can't walk on it for very long," she said. "No balance. I can't believe it."

"Aw, I'm sorry. I hope it feels better."

"Are you home?" she asked.

"Almost," I told her, though I was on my way to a restaurant to meet my roommate and some friends. Despite living more than a thousand miles away from me, she didn't like when I wasn't home. Something to worry about, I supposed, but really I didn't understand why she asked, why it mattered at all. We both had cell phones. We could talk anywhere.

"You should write about me," she said next. "You know, a young girl in the camps."

"I should?" I had forgotten that she'd mentioned this over our last phone call. The way she'd said it, it seemed like a passing thought and for me, it passed right through.

"How she survived. You could sell it."

"Yeah, uh, I'll think about it."

Bubbie and I never talked about the Holocaust, but now it was popping up on every other phone call. She wasn't pushy, stating the idea lightly, a casual suggestion, as if it had just come to her. I was caught off guard every time. She was usually so breezy when it came to the past. Were I to ask her for someone's name in an old photograph, she'd say, "Oh, they're dead," as if the person's mortality canceled out my interest. She cared much more about what was ahead—the next meal, the next holiday, the next time I was coming to visit her in Florida. She wanted to know how I was doing, how work was going, if I was staying warm. Nothing deep or involved or intense. And nothing about writing or war.

For decades, Bubbie avoided mentioning the war. Her close friends were refugees and survivors, already well acquainted with tragedy. They all had their own stories of loss and suffering, and no one wanted another. If the topic did come up, if someone asked her about where she was or what happened there, she chose a few select words, shook her head, and left it at that. With her children, she shared even less. She wanted them to set their sights forward, to look straight ahead. She decided early on that they'd lead very different lives from her. Better ones, with more safety and opportunity. The past would be irrelevant for them and maybe, possibly, the same might become true for her too. Silence, she figured, could function like a coat, like an extra large sweater, protection from the wind and cold.

Now she was inviting me to open that up, pull it apart stitch by stitch. I wasn't sure why. Would this be a destructive act? Or could it be helpful? The more I thought about what she was asking me to do, the more I felt the weight of her request. We'd be doing something no one in our family had ever done, unraveling the silence that surrounded us. The thought made me uneasy. There were countless ways to tell a story wrong, to mishandle a memory. Especially when the memory wasn't yours.

My own memories were uncomplicated. I could picture the swimming pool at Bubbie's old house in Michigan, the water pale and glassy blue, sun-speckled and shining, a diving board and slide off the far end. As a kid, I loved this pool. Scott jumped in the water straight away, but I always lowered myself in an inch at a time, grimacing and tiptoeing until the water felt just right. Once acclimated, I got back out and filled Bubbie's plastic watering can with a hose. My arm shook from its weight as I climbed the ladder rungs to the top of the slide. This was the height of childhood. I poured the water down and, taking a gulp of air, followed it myself, no longer timid or nervous or cold, no longer anything but free. I loved how my hair went flying, how my body spun around the curve of the slide and into the arms of the deep end. Bubbie watched from the side of the pool as she watered her plants, or from the kitchen, where she prepared our next meal. She was always cooking and baking. We visited every few months, making the five-hour drive between Chicago and Detroit. During

13

Passover, Scott and I snooped through her couch cushions and fabric scraps to find the afikoman. For Hanukkah, we sat with our cousins in a messy circle, opening presents with zeal. We got an inflatable raft one year and blew it up in the middle of Bubbie's living room, unable to wait for pool weather. I carried no sense of the dangers she faced as a child, the genocide she survived. Our lived experiences had so little overlap, they felt like parallel lines.

For months, Bubbie kept suggesting I write about her life. She wanted me to tell her story. I wasn't sure why or why now, but I knew why she wasn't going to do it herself. She couldn't read.

As someone who struggled with literacy, Bubbie was used to advocating for herself, making her voice known. It was a matter of necessity for her, the way in which she operated. She had to verbalize what she wanted to have any chance of getting it. And so she kept calling me, month after month, kept saying I should write her story.

The call that finally convinced me came in the middle of a weekday. I was re-writing ad copy at my desk when she called, a deadline staring me in the face. No one ever called me during work and I hesitated to answer. I was busy. But there was a part of me that wondered if it might be something important, something urgent. I decided to pick up, figuring the call wouldn't take too long, whatever it might be about. Our calls never did.

"Hello?" I answered.

"Wrong number," she said, hanging up with a click.

I burst into laughter, tears rolling down my cheeks. I was right, the call hadn't taken long at all.

Bubbie, I would later learn, had meant to call my brother Scott, and upon hearing the sound of my voice, knew I was not him. Had she been able to read her address book, she would have known who she was calling, but she couldn't and she didn't. So, click. Done. Call over.

Bubbie had no way to tell her own story. Like other Holocaust survivors, she struggled to find the right words, to express the full scope of what she'd endured during the war. But unlike most survivors, she also struggled with everyday matters, mundane tasks like dialing the right grandchild. She could speak six languages—English, German, Hebrew, Hungarian, Romanian and Yiddish (or Jewish, as she calls it)—but not read or write in any of them. Her ability to communicate was constantly being capped, in every encounter with a new person, every entrance to a new place. For her, writing her own story was not an option. If she wanted to be heard, she had to come up with something else. Something that might work differently, that might be more accommodating. It would be necessary to invent a new language.

Which was what she was trying to do. She was reaching out to me, her youngest child's youngest child, the one who liked to write, who called without having anything to say. She had played with me as a kid, watched me grow. She sent homemade pastries in the mail when we weren't together and showed me how to knead and roll the dough when we were. In junior high, as the ends of my favorite plaid pajama pants got ratty, she hemmed them into shorts for me. I wore those yellow-and-blue shorts everywhere. In my high school years, she sat on the sidelines of my varsity lacrosse games when she came in town to visit, supporting me despite not knowing a single rule to that sport or any other. I could never explain the details of my life to her, the activities and ambitions that filled my time. She was there anyway, watching from the edge, offering her support. Now she was asking me, in her own way, to do the same. All I had to do was show up.

The flight to Fort Lauderdale was rocky, miles of turbulence throttling me in my seat. When the plane landed, I peeled my hands off the armrests and let my lungs re-inflate. Near baggage claim, I caught an airport shuttle van to Bubbie's place, a half-hour ride from the airport. South Florida streamed through the van's dark tinted windows: extra-long strip malls along extra-wide streets, empty sidewalks dividing the two, palm trees hovering over the edges of traffic with yellow twinkle lights wrapped around their trunks as if they too were bushy evergreens up north. Everything felt strange to me. Surf & turf restaurants featured their owners' faces on the signs out front. Pre-schools stood next to adult daycare centers. In my grandma's town, there's an eleven-story statue of Pegasus off one of the main roads. At its base, the winged horse stomps on a dragon curled in the fetal position. Both animals' nostrils are flared out, the dragon gnashing its pointed teeth. It's the third-largest statue in the United States, this dragon-trampling Pegasus, not much smaller than the Statue of Liberty.

The shuttle van dropped me off in front of Bubbie's high-rise condo building, a broad-shouldered structure the same color as banana pudding. I slung my duffel bag over my shoulder and headed up to the fifteenth floor. No one is ever as excited to see me as Bubbie. As soon as I walked into her place, she threw her arms around me. "Brooke! My baby!" she said, giving me a squeeze and a peck on the cheek, her whole face alit. "Mwah," she added, in case I missed the message. I hugged her back, beaming, saying her name with an exclamation point too.

At five feet tall, Bubbie stood like a bull, stubborn and sure-footed. She spoke in excitable bursts and gave hugs that could swallow a person whole. There was an innate warmth to her, a liveliness and light. Her hair was always well coiffed, her hands decked with gold jewelry, nails shiny with polish. No matter where she went, she took a tube of lipstick with her. Best to be safe.

Bubbie's condo faced west, so you could smell the ocean but not see it. In the living room, I dropped my duffel bag by the off-white sectional that would serve as my bed for the next few days. The floors gleamed with slick tile, a canvas of white and off-white everywhere you looked. Mirrored walls reflected the main room back onto itself. Bubbie kept a pink beach towel over the cream-colored couch cushions, a leopard-print blanket over the neighboring armchair. Welcome to Florida, it all seemed to say. You made it.

Portraits of stony women hung on the walls, some painted, some stitched. In the corner of the room was her china cabinet, filled with figurines and family photos, my cousins and I as little kids, bad hair and confusing teeth. Beyond the cabinet was a sliding glass door that led to the balcony. I nearly tripped over a pile of cantaloupes trying to open it.

"Bubbie, why is there fruit on the floor?"

"The sun is good there," she said. "Leave them. They're ripening."

Who could argue with that? I navigated around the fruit and stepped out onto the balcony. This was my favorite part of her place. If you looked past all the oversized parking lots and glaring traffic lights, the view was serene: winding canals, leafy green palm trees, a few tiny boats bobbing in the water. Everything looks tiny from fifteen floors up. I could see why Bubbie liked living here. It was a rare perspective, towering but stable, sublime in its clarity and breadth.

Whereas others flew to Europe to learn about the war, Florida was always my end destination. I resisted the idea of visiting the camps, sites of devastation and death. My impulse was not to return to, but to run from, to sprint, head down, arms pumping. This much was clear to me. Two years earlier, I'd backpacked around Europe with a friend and considered visiting a concentration camp as part of the trip, but decided against it, not wanting to spend a full day in tears. I did not want a visceral experience, then or now, but a personal one. No one knew Bubbie's story better than she did, and here, in Florida, was where she'd made her home. Here, by the water. Here, by the strip mall. Here, by the giant winged horse statue. My family history was not being preserved in Europe, in death camps and memorials, in archives and shadows and stones, but here, in swampy south Florida.

I had no idea what we were about to do. Was she ready? Was I? I didn't want to hurt her and feared I might. The past always seemed so dangerous to me, forbidden even, a place we didn't dare venture. Certainly there was a reason for everyone's silence. I didn't know how much she could handle, how far I could or should push. Would my questions tear the sutures holding everything together? I took a breath of sea air, briny and sharp. There was only one way to find out.

That night, we recorded our first interview together. Bubbie sat in her armchair wearing a floral top and dark slacks while I sat pretzel-like on the couch next to her in a climbing tee and shorts. I wanted to interview her somewhere where she was comfortable, at ease in, even if it was full of distractions. Her living room proved to be exactly that. Between the two of us was an end table stocked with vitamin bottles, tissues, old photos, a portable phone and a jar of nuts, each its own diversion. I set my laptop on a dining-room chair on the other side of the room and opened the video app on my computer, adjusting the screen to make sure we were both in frame. I wasn't sure why that mattered, but it felt right.

"OK," I said, hitting the red button and skittering back to the couch. This was it, what I'd flown to south Florida for, what she'd been suggesting on all those phone calls over all those months. I looked at her with nervous, expectant eyes. "It's recording."

TWO

— Hmm?

— It's recording.

— Recording? I'm very grateful that you came, Brooke. And I love having you.

— Thank you.

— And I wish we can see more of you guys. Mom is coming after Christmas? That'd be nice. I don't know for how long. That'd be nice to have her.

— You're sneaking a little guilt trip in there right away.

— And I think Scott might come. I hope so.

— Can you tell me about when you were a little girl?

— Hmm?

— When you were a little kid?

— I am born in Czechoslovakia. It records it?

— It's still recording, yeah.

— People come to visit. And I grow up little by little. And then we moved to Maramoset-Sighet. So we lived in Sighet. Till the Nazis came. All kinds of stories you hear, what happens in the city, what happens here, what happened there. The Nazis are everywhere. All the grown-up people talking about it. Scary.

— Did you understand it?

— Yeah. And before you know, the Nazis came down the street. And in every house, they take. They tell all the Jews, Out of the house, get out of the house. In German. You must leave your house. Get out. Leave nothing in your hands. Don't take nothing. Get out. And line up in five. Five people, in the street. Line up. One house, another house, everybody had to empty the house. Leave no kids, no grandpa, nobody. Just go. Line up. So house to house, they did. And we had to go line up and go, go, go until the end. And by the end, we had to turn right on the main street. And everybody walking down, Oh my gosh, what's gonna happen to us? What's going on? My goodness. Unbelievable. They are so scared. We kept on walking, we had to walk.

We stopped at the synagogue, a big synagogue was on the right-hand side. Huge. And they said, Everybody go in the synagogue. Take a seat and take off all your gold, all your belongings and throw them in the middle in the, you know, front yard. Everyone had to throw everything out. The earrings, rings, necklace— everything. Everything of value we had to throw down there. And people scared and scared and scared. And crying. What's gonna happen to us? What's gonna happen to us? Nothing to eat, nothing to drink. What's gonna happen? We can't even go in the toilet. Unbelievable. We are so many people here in…the big building. Everybody complaining, complaining, another day go by, another day go by. And then the Nazis come. Everybody, heraus! Come out and line up. Come out! Yelling, you know. What they did. People come out from the synagogue one by one and leaving all the belongings, what they had on, leaving in the middle of the front yard. Then we kept walking and walking. Where are you walking? To the train station.

THREE

Bubbie used unbelievable as a filler word, the way I used uh or um. Unbelievable, she said of my on-time arrival at the airport. Unbelievable, she said of the produce selection at the grocery store. Unbelievable, she said of the war that wiped out her family. Once the worst has happened, everything becomes hard to believe.

After I settled into Bubbie's condo, I offered to help her run some errands. Her cell phone had been lost or stolen the week before—the jury was still out on which one it was—and Bubbie needed a new one. She said yes right away, grabbing a light jacket from her closet as well as the black metal cane my mom was trying to get her to use. Her balance had been getting worse lately, shakier with age. She tossed me the keys to her car and we left the condo, the cane tucked high under her arm. It hovered a foot or two above the ground the whole way to the parking garage.

Bubbie owned her own car, but my mom had recently convinced her not to get behind the wheel anymore. It was no longer safe, for her or others. Enter me, the grandkid who likes to write and can also drive. Throughout my trip to Florida, Bubbie had me drive more miles and run more errands than I ever could have predicted. Within hours of my arrival, we drove to the AT&T store, bought her a new cell phone, stopped at a flea market, swung by the grocery store, got stuck in traffic, tried (and failed) to get gas, and went to a nearby restaurant to eat. Over lunch, she told me she wanted to get her hair done. Then she said never mind.

"Are you sure?" I didn't mind taking her to the salon. Nothing could be as bad as the AT&T store. If anything it'd give me a chance to catch my breath.

"Yeah, you know how I look. And I look good."

I smiled at that. She always spoke with such confidence, such certainty. I admired how she knew what she wanted and went for it. She was dauntless in a way that seemed impossible to me. She said what she meant, and said it straight.

Later that night, she changed her mind again.

We didn't have time to make an appointment, so Bubbie and I agreed to go first thing in the morning. After breakfast, we drove to the salon, part of a strip mall nearby. I dropped her off and left to find a gas station. Though I had tried to fill the tank the day before, the gas pump hadn't worked. This time, while checking my email at the pump, I realized why: a credit card skimmer had stolen my identity. I finished filling the car with gas, paid, then froze my account. Ah, Florida.

The hair salon was a long, open-concept space with skinny fluorescent bulbs that hung from the ceiling. Lines of black styling chairs ran along the walls. The chairs, mostly empty, were turned in every direction. My hope was that Bubbie was still near the beginning of her appointment so I could sit down and sort through the charges on my card. An older man sat slumped in a styling chair on the left side. Across from him, a younger, wiry-haired woman was getting her bangs trimmed. I looked around the stark salon, then looked again.

Bubbie wasn't there.

I asked the lady behind the front counter if she had seen my grandma, but the woman gave me a half-hearted shrug. She couldn't recall. Dumbfounded as to where Bubbie might have gone, I tried calling her on her brand-new cell phone. My call went straight to voicemail. The phone wasn't even on.

I walked up and down the strip mall looking for Bubbie. She couldn't have gone far, and yet she was nowhere in sight. I peeked around the back of the salon and in the parking lot. She wasn't there. I had no clue where she might have gone—she was not a particularly agile or mobile person. Did she walk somewhere else? Get lost? Find another place for a haircut? There were no other salons in the strip mall, and the corner pet groomer seemed like a stretch.

I was getting nervous. Normally grandparents lose their grandchildren and not the other way around. Where was Bubbie? And how did I lose her?

Bubbie was always on the move, always keeping busy. She was go, go, go, all day long. While I was happy to take a nap on the couch or stretch out with a book, Bubbie never sat still. She filled every pocket of time with activity, letting no moment pass her by. She visited her neighbors, cooked, shopped, cleaned, played cards, called friends, did laundry, and walked laps in her building's swimming pool. A woman who survives stays surviving.

One afternoon, a neighbor knocked on Bubbie's door. Bubbie opened it and the woman handed her a large bouquet of flowers, leaving after less than a minute of small talk. I watched the exchange from the couch. As Bubbie looked for a vase in the kitchen, I asked her who the lady at the door was and she told me she didn't know her name. Right. Okay. So, why did she bring a bouquet?

Apparently this neighbor had been bedridden the week prior with a leg injury. When Bubbie found out, she went out of her way to cook and deliver homemade food for the woman, never bothering to ask for details, like what happened to her leg or how she was feeling or if she had a particular name she liked to go by. Bubbie was a deeply generous person in this way. She didn't need to be asked or told because she was always at the ready. Ready to act, ready to give, ready to take charge and take care of things. People who were otherwise boring to her became interesting when ill. They gave her something to do, and there was nothing she liked more than having something to do. Her hands were especially keen on staying busy. They were always peeling, stirring, baking, dialing, sweeping, washing, turning, cleaning, fixing—something. With Bubbie, it was always something. She was a tireless person, through and through.

Only at night, when everything fell quiet and there was nothing for her hands to peel or stir or bake, no friends to visit or neighbors to feed, no pools to pad through or grocery stores to peruse, only then would she lose this ceaseless forward motion. She would turn off the lights in her condo one by one and get into her bed backwards with her feet at the head of the bed and her head at the foot. She believed there was more air in the middle of the room and wanted to get as much as she could. She fluffed her pillow, laid her head upon it and slid into the ever-pressing past. She couldn't help it. Even the most tireless people get tired sometime. At night, as the sky swelled with darkness and the ocean went black, the war caught hold of her. It did not let go.

That's what she called what happened—the war. It summed everything up: all the suffering, all the loss. The bedlam, the bloodshed, the frozen toes. She had to learn the word Holocaust later like everybody else. She had to learn a whole new language. The words she knew were never enough.

At night, she went to bed and the war tucked her in. She laid in her nightgown with thoughts of those who didn't make it swimming in her head. She wondered what they would have looked like had they lived, how they would've bloomed and grown. She kept her eyes closed and tried to mold their soft faces into handsome, striking forms, but the images were slippery. Late at night, hoping for sleep, she forgot what she most wanted to remember and remembered what she most wanted to forget. The war did not allow otherwise. She saw her old town, her old house, a flood of childhood memories, and the heavy truth of what brought about their abrupt and violent end. It came to her in flashes, in jagged shards, the edges brutally sharp.

Throughout the night, waves of sadness, fear and anger came over her, but more than anything, what she felt was alone. She survived when so many people she knew and loved did not. Their memory was all but lost, left for her alone to keep, to carry through the world. It was a burden she had known for the majority of her life. How much she'd have loved to talk to them again, to sit together and see their cheery faces. To go back to before the madness began, before the destruction and chaos. She sunk into her bed and let herself wish for things that could never be. Undos, redos. Rewinds. Resurrections. One more meal together. One more story. A story with a happy ending, cozy and warm. Or maybe no ending at all, a non-ending to set things right. She drifted into restless sleep with the impossible as her cover. How different things could have been. It was a dangerous thought and she tried her best not to think it. But there it was, in the darkness, night after night, waiting.

In the morning, Bubbie pushed her grief and sorrow back below the surface. She buried it deep, readying herself to pick up wherever she'd left off the day before. And pick up she did. The sun streamed in through the windows and she found a litany of household chores to do. She took charge and moved fast, always trying to get ahead, to outpace the pain of memory. Stillness was not in her nature. She spent her time finding people to take care of, problems to solve, blankets to fold, cookies to bake, pans to scrub, cabinets to dust, pants to hem. A feeling couldn't reach you if it couldn't find you. And for the most part, her method worked. It was effective. She thought of other things, tackled other tasks. She had been at it for years. Her hands peeled and stirred and baked and dialed and swept and washed and turned and cleaned, and every other busying action, too. People gave her flowers for it.

There, finally, across the way, I spotted Bubbie. She was at the far end of the strip mall, sitting in front of Publix (the giant chain grocery store) on a motorized scooter that was not hers. I jogged over, relieved to find her. It turned out that the hair salon had been closed when I'd first dropped her off there, so she had moved to the grocery store to make it easier for me to find her. But why would sitting in front of the grocery store make anything easier? How would I have ever thought to look there? It didn't make any sense to me. The grocery store was nowhere near the hair salon. And where did she get that scooter she was sitting on? I hoped she didn't steal it, but also didn't ask. I helped Bubbie up, her cane forgotten back at the condo, and we walked arm in arm to the salon.

For the second time in ten minutes, I went up to the front counter. A few more people had filled the black styling chairs since I had last been in, searching for Bubbie.

"You find her?" the lady at the front desk asked me.

Already this simple task had turned into a small fiasco. I was happy to finally be getting it right.

"Yes," I told the lady. "She's with me now. And she'd like to get her hair done."

And yet, from the corner of my eye, I could see that she was not with me. Not any more. Bubbie had pushed past the front desk, walking through the salon, already in the back by the shampoo station. I called for her, but she didn't respond, either because she was a headstrong bull of a woman or an older person with bad hearing. It was hard to say. I finished talking with the lady at the front, adding Bubbie's name to the waitlist, then tracked her down.

"Bubbie, the lady said we have to wait. No one is available yet."

"I already ask. This lady will wash my hair."

A tall stylist smiled at me as she pulled a black nylon cape from a high shelf. Her hair was tied up in an even taller bun. Another stylist walked by us, a Latina woman with brassy highlights. "Come to my station when you're done, OK sweetie?" Bubbie gave her a nod.

I was baffled. You're not supposed to barge in and demand people do things for you. That's not how things get done. And yet there was Bubbie, head in a porcelain sink, a professional's hands in her hair, getting things done.

Unbelievable, I muttered, mostly to myself.

FOUR

Čierna nad Tisou was a small railway town in the corner of what was then Czechoslovakia, now Slovakia. Hundreds of train tracks cut through the town, an intersection near the borders of Czechoslovakia, Hungary, Romania and Poland. Golda Indig (née Feuerwerger) was born there in 1930, the fifth of seven children. The siblings, as Golda tells it, arrived in alternating order: a girl, a boy, a girl, a boy and so on. Suri was the eldest daughter and Bumme the eldest son. Next came Blimchu, a girl, and Mechel, a boy. The youngest of the lot were Golda, Meilekh, and Rojha Blima. The children all had soft brown hair and big, expressive eyes, their faces round and flush like their parents. They knew nothing of bigotry or violence or Nazis.

Henia, their mom, was a slender woman with dark brown eyes and fair skin. She took care of the children, mending their socks when they tore holes in them and cooking their meals when their stomachs growled. Throughout the day, she sang to the kids around the house, her voice a balm to their young worries and fears. She too had come from a big traditional Jewish family and loved having one of her own. Motherhood filled her with a sense of purpose and pride. She was very good at it.

But motherhood also came with heartache. Months either before or after giving birth to Golda—the exact timing now unknown—Henia noticed something wrong with her eldest child Suri, then nine years old. One visit with the doctor confirmed it: Suri had pneumonia. Henia watched as her daughter grew pale and weak, her small body fixed under the covers of her bed, a fragment of her former self. Soon, Suri died. The whole family mourned the loss, but Henia was especially grief-stricken. Her firstborn, her baby girl, was gone. As she took care of the rest of her brood, including young Golda, she made sure to keep a close eye out for signs of illness and disease. She could not bear to lose another part of her family.

While Henia was busy caring for the children and the house, Golda's father Peretz worked in town. Peretz was a cattle dealer, selling and moving cows as needed. He bartered, made deals and tended to the animals. He was good with animals and enjoyed their company. In the wintertime, he worked as a woodcutter, chopping down trees and transporting the logs. Once processed, the wood heated all the homes in the area. Golda remembers watching from a window in their house as the logs were sent down the river to the lumber mill. The men moved the wood along the water, letting it float through a thicket of forest and snow.

For Golda, this was a simple and happy time. She watched her dad take care of the family's animals, a sturdy cow and two horses. She helped her mom with chores around the house and tagged along with her older brothers and sister. All throughout the day they played games together both inside the house and out in the yard. Golda picked up all sorts of fun and silly tricks from her siblings, like the one where she'd stand in the corner of a room and wrap her arms around herself to make it look like she was kissing a mysterious stranger. She was a playful little girl, happy and joyful, with a mischievous side too. When riled up, she could be a spitfire. Once, after her older brothers Bumme and Mechel told her she couldn't play with their ball, she decided to hide it from them so they couldn't play with it either. She stuck the ball inside the family's wood stove and promptly forgot about it. Later in the day, as her mom began to prepare dinner, the whole house filled with a horrible stench. Henia opened the stove door and saw a half-melted ball before her. No one suspected it had been little, lovable Goldie.

Like everyone in her family, Golda adored her dad the most. He was a cheerful man, always whistling around the house and yard. When he came home from a day's work, either with the cattle or with scores of timber, she and her siblings rushed to the door to greet him. At dinner, she snuck onto his lap and finished eating her meal from there. Every so often, the family visited Peretz's mother Malka, who was a widow living on her own by then. Malka's house was a half-day trek away and getting there required two horses and a carriage. Peretz looked forward to these trips, as difficult as they were. Golda did, too. She revered her grandma.

When the family arrived at Malka's home, she welcomed them in, feeding everyone right away. She was a talented cook. Later, she sat the children down and told them exciting, fanciful tales, tales that brought them to the edges of their seats, tales they couldn't resist. Her stories starred a warm and wise grandmother who lived in a cottage with her twelve grandchildren and wore a long skirt they could all hide underneath should they get scared. The kids in her stories faced threats of danger, dark spots in the woods and wild, frightening creatures, but they were always kept safe by their quick-thinking grandmother, her sweeping skirt the ultimate image of safety and comfort. She came through for them, not by strength or force, but through clever plans and magical aids. Malka loved telling these tales to her grandchildren and Golda loved hearing them. She could not get enough. The action, the suspense, the way things always seemed to work out in the end. Golda enjoyed her grandma's Bubbie Beitzah stories so much that she never forgot them, holding onto them for decades until she could regale her own kids and grandkids—my cousins, my brother and me.

More than tall tales, what Golda treasured was spending time with Malka. At home she had to vie for attention, but with her grandma, there was no shortage. Her love was infinite. Malka chatted with her, sang to her and let Golda sleep in her bed. They took walks outside together, Malka always ready with a loaf or two of challah tucked into her skirt's pockets should they get hungry. She taught Golda things no one else did, like how to turn water, butter, salt and flour into delicious pastry dough. She pulled a chair up to the kitchen table so Golda could reach it, and showed her how to use a rolling pin, transforming a lump of dough into a paper-thin sheet for filling and folding. They stuffed their cookies and crescent rolls with more sweets, often sugar-drenched walnuts or raisins or jam, sealing them with a press of their fingers. Sometimes Golda's older sister Blimchu would join them in the kitchen and sometimes it'd just be them, Malka and Golda, baking elbow to elbow. The smell of the cookies danced in the air around them.

When Golda was six years old, everything changed. Tragedy fell upon her family in a swift series of events, one after another. It unsteadied them all. And it was only the beginning.

First came the move. Henia was worried about her father, a widower living on his own. He was getting older and she fretted over his health, his ability to care for himself. If pneumonia could take her eldest daughter's life, perhaps it'd come for her father too. She stressed over how far away she was from him, and how little help she could offer from there. Henia's father still lived in the town where she had grown up, only now he was all alone and prone to illness. She knew that if the family was nearby, she could be his caregiver if and when the time came for such a thing. She wanted nothing more than to be close to him again. Peretz agreed.

The family of eight packed up their belongings. They headed south to Henia's hometown, a bigger city in a bigger country, to see out their plan. They left Czechoslovakia and without knowing, left the country for good. No one in the family but Henia would ever return.

I need to make a small caveat here. Golda was six years old when her family left Czechoslovakia. Her understanding of why they moved was that of a child. There's no way to say if Henia's worries about her father were the only reason for their move, or simply the only reason my grandma knew. She may have been remembering her mother's motivations accurately, or she may have never truly known them. The timeline leaves a few questions. Again and again, throughout the gathering of my grandma's story, I was met with uncertainty in the face of all these half-known truths. Why did so-and-so do that? How did such-and-such happen? When? With whom? Some details, I came to find, could not be fact-checked. Some details simply die when those who know them do.

◆

Sighet—nestled in the rolling hills off the Tisza River, encircled by the Carpathian Mountains, claimed at different times by Hungary and Romania—was a bustling, close-knit community. With its sawmills and salt mines, the town was a center for forestry and the salt trade. Small shops, taverns and schools lined the wide, open streets with farmlands right outside its borders. Nearly 14,000 Jews called Sighet home. Insulated by mountains and river, they remained culturally secluded from much of modern Europe, carrying out a traditional way of life that went back centuries. They had their own Hebrew presses and libraries, and followed their own religious leaders. They worked as craftsmen, coachmen, laborers and shopkeepers. If this small Romanian town sounds at all familiar to you, it's most likely because of an observant, brown-haired boy who lived there, a boy named Elie Wiesel, who became friends with Golda's brother Mechel after the family moved to town, and later went on to become an author, activist, professor and Nobel Peace Prize recipient. His book *Night*, published in English in 1960, sold millions of copies around the world, becoming "a touchstone for countless readers, for whom it was likely their first encounter with Holocaust literature."[1] This was true for me. In eighth grade, I read *Night* in English class, the first book on the Holocaust I'd ever come across. The book opens in Sighet before the war has reached the town. My eyes turned into searchlights as I read, pouring over the pages, desperate to spot Golda and her family in the text. Perhaps she might appear at the school, I thought, or with her brother Mechel, or maybe there'd be a quick passing on the street, a subtle mention. I wanted to see what had always been obscured from me, to glimpse what no longer was. I wanted to look away too, my stomach hard with dread.

Wiesel's words gripped me. As I reached the last page, I realized I'd found Golda's family but only in one phrase: the Jews of Sighet.

Golda's family became part of the Jews of Sighet when they moved into a large corner house in town. The house was split into three units—one for Golda's grandfather, one for her cousin's family and one for her own. An apple tree and a well for water sat in the backyard, drawing neighbors over on a regular basis. The move also drew Golda closer to her paternal grandmother Malka, whose house she could now walk to in a little over an hour. Without needing her parents, a carriage and horses, she was free to visit more often, baking more pastries and hearing more stories of wolves, wonder and elderly heroines.

In the end, it was not Golda's grandfather who fell ill but her own father. Peretz must have known something was off with his health back in Czechoslovakia and thought having more family around would be a good idea if he were proven right. He went to a nearby hospital to figure out what was going on with his body, but the doctors couldn't find anything wrong with him. It wasn't pneumonia. He traveled to a more established hospital further away. This time the doctors found the issue. It was prostate cancer and it was serious.

Golda's dad started spending long spans of time away from the family, lying flat in a narrow hospital bed. He received an exhausting amount of medical treatment. Nothing seemed to help and he quickly grew reedy, his face sallow and gaunt. No one could believe a person so strong could be so sick. He was the cattleman, he was the lumberjack. A horse had once bucked him in the chest, sending him flying backwards, and he'd popped up like it was nothing. The man was invincible. And now he was dying. His cheeks became caverns, his eyes heavy stones. On an otherwise calm and normal day, Peretz died. The family's sole provider, the man they all adored, the man who loved to whistle, who turned his lap into a chair for his children, was gone. He was thirty-six years old.

Golda and her family were devastated. Their eight was now seven. Without Peretz, the leader of their little band, they all felt lost. Golda's grandma Malka could not stop crying. She wailed out loud, asking why, why, why, over and over, wishing it had been her and not her beloved son. Her words rang in Golda's ears. The local synagogue held a funeral for Peretz, but Golda was not allowed to attend. The adults in her life deemed her too young for the service. Instead, she stayed at home and watched from the window as six men, strong like her father had been, carried his body away on a wooden board, a thin linen laid carefully over top. A flock of mourners dressed in black followed the procession down the street, her grandma Malka still crying, still asking why, why.

After Peretz's passing, nothing was the same. Sadness surrounded the family. Golda's mom Henia was consumed with grief. Peretz had been her anchor, her love, the man she'd built her life around. When someone suggested she get remarried, she refused, repelled by the thought that the father of her children could in any way be replaced. It was unthinkable to her. Instead, she decided she would support the family on her own, despite never having had a job before. She made up her mind on the matter, and that was that. The family would move on from the loss by themselves, survive despite it. She would lead the way.

Henia started working long days as a traveling merchant. She trudged from one city to the next, buying and selling items, finding sales wherever she could. Often her travels took her out of the country, going back and forth between Romania, Hungary and Czechoslovakia. (During this time, the borders moved; Hungary took control of Sighet from Romania, and with it the rest of Northern Transylvania.) Henia kept traveling, selling sewing supplies like zippers, threads, fabrics and trimmings. Many women designed and sewed their family's clothes at the time, so the market was a wide one.

While Henia was away on business, her younger sister Suri, named as her eldest daughter once was, helped out around the house. To the kids, Aunt Suri was kind and gentle, quick to clean up a mess but not to scold anyone for making it. She watched the younger kids while her sister was away, caring for the children, feeding them, keeping them busy and safe.

Meanwhile, the older kids either went to school or got jobs. Mechel and Golda, being two years apart, went to the same middle school. In the morning, they walked to class together and in the afternoon, they split. Mechel went to yeshiva, a secondary religious school that only allowed boys, while Golda returned to the house to help out with chores. With her mom traveling so much, there was more for her to do at home.

When I asked Bubbie how many years she was in school, she told me four. This meant that for several years before the war—which ones, I cannot say—she did not attend school at all. Instead she spent her days with Malka, cooking and cleaning. I wish I knew more about her education, how it differed from that of her siblings, when and why her family held her back. I wish I knew more because I did not understand why it was that she could not read. The vast majority of Holocaust survivors were literate, something I only learned late in high school. Even

Bubbie's closest friends, women with similar backgrounds and experiences, could read. She was the exception, not the rule. Why, I wondered, was reading so difficult for her? What made literacy so elusive?

Such questions are easier to ask than they are to answer. Golda struggled with reading because her dad had died, her world spun on its head. She struggled because she may have had a learning disability. She struggled because she wasn't in class in the first place. (She wasn't in class because her dad had died? Because her grandma was grieving? Because Golda was a girl, the expectations set elsewhere? I was unsure about this too.) Later, Golda struggled because of the war. Because imprisonment, because statelessness, because starvation. She struggled because trauma affects the brain in profound and complex ways. Golda struggled because Golda struggled. When she was in school, she was a step behind her peers, trying her best to follow along. When she wasn't in school, she fell even further behind. From what I knew, Mechel did not miss class and did not struggle.

While the middle two siblings went to school (or not), the eldest of the bunch, Bumme and Blimchu, were sent to work in Budapest. To help make ends meet at home, they got jobs at a bakery in the city—Blimchu cracking nuts, Bumme making pastries—sending what little money they made back to their mom. In Budapest, Bumme took on the role of protector, watching out for his sister both at work and afterwards, as his father would have done. Much had fallen on his young shoulders upon the death of his dad. When the siblings returned to Sighet, Blimchu went back to helping out around the house while Bumme picked up an apprenticeship at a local bakery. He was the youngest person to work there and was assigned the most demanding physical tasks. He baked through the night, every night, bringing a fresh loaf of bread home in the morning. The rest of the family split the bread, eating while Bumme slept, or tried to sleep amid their noise. Come nightfall, he left for the bakery to do it all again. Despite his fatigue, he enjoyed the job. He liked the feeling of working with his hands and providing for his mother and siblings, of feeding them and filling his father's shoes.

Like Bumme, everyone in the family had a role to play—working in town, cooking at home, milking the cow, cleaning the house. Golda was put in charge of washing floors and peeling potatoes for dinner. The whole family struggled and strived like this, push and pull, finding ways to make things work. They met new people, made new friends. Bumme got engaged to his girlfriend. Blimchu went out with her friends more and more, a full-blown teenager with an active social life. Golda tried to tag along, but her four-years-older sister always turned her down. Instead, Golda had sleepovers at her grandma Malka's house, talking and baking with her for hours. They were as close as they could be. Mechel continued with his studies, balancing both school and yeshiva. Aunt Suri cared for the little ones, Meilekh and Rojha Blima, playing with them around the house. Henia continued to travel, selling sewing supplies to women in the surrounding areas. For additional income, she sold the surplus milk their cow produced. They all looked for ways to help. They scrubbed and worked and scavenged and shared and studied and baked. However they could, the family got by.

When rumors filtered into town of far-off violence, men with guns and helmets making demands, streets strewn with broken glass and bloodstains to match, they all deemed it unlikely to come to Sighet, their quiet town, tucked behind the Tisza River. It couldn't be. It wouldn't. Even as Bumme was called into the Hungarian Labor Service, a conscription for all Jewish men of age to serve as forced laborers for the state, they did not believe the worst of what they had heard. Surely such persecution was not possible, not here, not now. How could it be? Bumme left home for forced labor on the Eastern Front and the seven became six.

The only thing Golda ever saw out of the ordinary was on a walk home with Malka. They passed by the school and saw a teacher through the window, a former friend of her father's, hanging. Malka told her not to look, averting her eyes. It was a suicide. Golda never made any connection between this instance and the war, and it's quite possible there was none. It's only me who wonders.

Word spread through Sighet that the war was going to end soon and people were pleased. Everything would calm again. Everything would be all right. The men would return. For Golda and her family, things seemed okay. They had been moving on from their losses, finding their footing just fine. Germany occupied Hungary and two Jewish ghettos were formed in town, a small one and a large one, and still they did not understand what was happening. Their house was within the ghetto boundaries, so they did not have to move. Everything was all right. Everything was the same. Until one day, in the spring of 1944, when it very much wasn't.

FIVE

— They put everyone in the train. Like cattle, pushed us in. All of us. Full. Lot of people. On one train, the next train. We were full, full of people there. Again no nothing to drink, nothing to eat, we can't even go in the bathroom. *Everybody, quiet! Sit down!* You know, scary. Nothing you can do. We had to go in and sit down. So many people you can hardly sit in the train. It's like cattle, you know. Pushed us in. And what happened? Kept on going and going on the train, I don't know how many days we went on the train, till we arrived at Auschwitz.

They said come down from the train, one by one, line up. And then they say, you go right, you go left. Unbelievable. Who go left goes to the crematorium. They didn't say it, but we smelled it later. We went to the right, we had to shower. Walk in disinfecting water first and then we go shower. And they gave us one grey dress, that's all we ever had. A grey dress. And then they cut everybody's hair off. That was a big shock to everybody. Take the hair off too.

— They shaved you bald?

— Bald.

— All the way?

— For a long time. Until we grow it back. And it was terrible to go through with that too. But what can you do? We had to go in line and do it. We kept on walking with the grey dress and line up, line up. Till they took us to another building. I don't know how many hundreds and hundreds and hundreds of people were there. And they put us in a small place, fourteen people to each little hole had to go in and lay down like herring! We were like herring laying on top of one another. We can't complain, we can't say nothing.

There was a Polish lady. She said: *Shhh. Be quiet. If not, they gonna send you too. To the crematorium. See that? You smell that? Your families, they burning there!*

That's what they used to tell us.

Your family is burning there!

Nothing we could do. Be quiet, be quiet, be quiet. Three o'clock in the morning, we have to get up. *Line up. Five in a row, line up, line up.* They were whistling to go out. And it was cold, terrible cold. And we went there, under the building, we lined up. And that what it was. Shivering, shivering. They brought us coffee for six people, to drink from it. A little bit. What was in the coffee? Poison. So the girls cannot have their period. You know, stop everything from being normal. *Drink that, drink that.* You have to drink and share it with other people there. *Drink, drink. All of it, drink it up.* And that was our breakfast, drinking the black coffee. And then we went back in the block, everybody back in the same place. We were back for quite a few days. And every morning we have to get up with the whistle, you know, they whistle, they holler, *Everybody get up and line up under the building.* All of us. Scared, shaking like a leaf. And again they give us coffee. *Drink up that coffee, that's all you gonna get for breakfast. Nothing else.* And we had to do what they tell us.

After two three days, she said, *Line up, I'm taking you to the bathroom.* The bathroom, what was? A big hole and a big piece of wood, maybe a little wider than that.

All the way across. Long. And you go do your business. *Everybody, line up and do it. When they're done, come back to the roll.* That's what happened. It happened again and again like that. Every other day. They took us out to do that. In the meantime, they didn't give us to eat.

Finally, they brought something to eat in a big bowl. Six people eat from one bowl. No spoon, we eat like a dog. That's how they gave us. And we couldn't say another word. *Share it. And be quiet. You know what's happening. They gonna take you out to get burned if you make noise.*

And we kept on doing that. Then they send us out from the building. *Let's go, line up. Everybody line up, line up.* And what did we do? We line up.

SIX

Systematic mass murder is a delicate business. It requires a clear, horrific vision; merciless indoctrination; and excellent organizational skills. Unquestioning minds help. Eager participants, the seeds of anger and fear, hunger for a scapegoat. The Nazis formalized their plan for genocide in eighty-five minutes. At the meeting, known as the Wannsee Conference, they did not use words like murder or extermination, but said "labor deployment" and "supervision" and "natural reduction." They said "final remnant" and "dealt with appropriately."[2] Rather than send the Jews to Madagascar, an earlier idea of theirs, or commit mass killings in ravines, vans, trenches and forests as they'd already done in Ukraine, the Nazis developed a new scheme. They planned to evict all of Europe's Jews, rob them of their belongings and deport them to concentration camps where they could be worked and killed away from the public eye. Evict, rob, deport, kill. The word genocide came later, coined by Polish Jewish lawyer Raphael Lemkin in 1944. It was meant to denote the destruction of an ethnic group or people, to better describe the scale and scope of the atrocities that the Nazis and their collaborators were committing.

Words have always fascinated me. They function as portals, entry points into other worlds. As a kid, I read every night before bed, eager to absorb as many words as I could. I wanted to immerse myself in the spaces they created, the perspectives they unveiled, otherwise not visible in the rest of my life. As an adult, I made them my work, becoming a copywriter for a living. I created new words for product and brand names and combined them constantly, forming taglines, headlines, supporting copy. Words transported me to new ideas, new thinking and feelings and places and jobs. Now I hoped they might take me back towards the past, that language could help trace the trauma to its roots. I had never looked so closely before, perhaps knowing how much suffering and sadness I'd have to confront. Words can separate us or they can bind us, and for Bubbie and me, I suspected they did both.

Abe Foxman, a Holocaust survivor born in Poland, spoke on the power of language in a Holocaust education campaign called #ItStartedWithWords. "The crematoria, gas chambers in Auschwitz and elsewhere, did not begin with bricks," Foxman said. "It began with words...evil words, hateful words, antisemitic words, words of prejudice. And they were permitted to proceed to violence because of the absence of words."[3] Words could lead the way to genocide, and silence could let it happen.

Nazi rhetoric planted ideas of racial purity and superiority of Germans over Jews, who made up less than one percent of the German population. The Nazis used language to classify and dehumanize the Jewish people, making it easier to discriminate against them later on. Propaganda referred to Jews as vermin, lice and other pests, explicitly declaring them as more animal than human. A 1935 issue of the German paper *Der Stürmer*, for example, featured a caricature of a Jewish man as a snake, his body adorned with stars of David, being choked by a giant white hand. It was captioned: *Don't let go!*[4] When this paper was released in Germany, my grandma was four years old and living in another country.

At other times, Nazi language was coded, relying on more subtle euphemisms to convey the message. These words were no less dangerous. The Final Solution, for example, framed the existence of Jews as a question, a problem, letting the word solution stand in for murder. In many documents, the Nazis used vague phrasing to make their hatred more bureaucratic in tone, more banal. Killing was called Sonderbehandlung, the German word for special treatment. In some places, it was shortened to S.B. By not calling their actions by name, they could obfuscate their intentions, deceive those affected, and claim innocence later. Some Nazi leaders worried their euphemisms were still too obvious. Partway through the war, they decided to change their language again. This time, they did not say that the Jews received special treatment, but that they were guided through the camps. As the magnitude of their war crimes intensified, the Nazis bent their language even further to mask it.

Even the word to describe this kind of hate is steeped in hate. In 2015, the International Holocaust Remembrance Alliance (IHRA), an intergovernmental body that advocates for Holocaust education and research, released a memo about antisemitism—not the concept but the spelling. Anti-Semitism, the more common way to spell the term at the time, was rooted in racist ideologies, pre-Nazi thinking. "The hyphenated spelling," the IHRA explained, "allows for the possibility of something called 'Semitism', which not only legitimizes a form of pseudo-scientific racial classification...but also divides the term, stripping it from its meaning of opposition and hatred toward Jews."[5]

The notion of "Semitism" comes from Semitic languages, a family of Middle Eastern languages including Arabic, Aramaic, Hebrew, Maltese, Tigrinya and more. Though linguistically related, these languages stem from different groups of people, each with their own history and heritage. There is no one Semitic people. But when German journalist Wilhelm Marr coined the term *Antisemitismus* in 1879, he used it to refer specifically to anti-Jewish campaigns, giving the discrimination a racial underpinning, a pseudo-scientific justification. The phrase caught on with anti-Jewish political movements keen to bolster their supremacist views with faulty science and fancy phrases. It was antisemitic by design.

"The unhyphenated spelling is favored by many scholars and institutions in order to dispel the idea that there is an entity [called] 'Semitism' which 'anti-Semitism' opposes," the IHRA stated in their 2015 memo. "Antisemitism should be read as a unified term so that the meaning of the generic term for modern Jew-hatred is clear...it is urgent that there is clarity and no room for confusion or obfuscation."

And yet, there was so much confusion and obfuscation, both past and present, externally and within myself. I wanted to write about my grandma and her life, but found myself digging into issues of orthography, etymology, race, religion, discrimination, policy, legal frameworks, bad science, good branding. Words, powerful as they were, could obscure as much as they illuminated. A year after their memo on the spelling of antisemitism, the IHRA created a working definition for the word—"a certain perception of Jews, which may be expressed as hatred toward Jews"[6]— that was so broad, more than a hundred Israeli and international civil organizations wrote a letter to the UN Secretary-General in April 2023 to ask that the UN not adopt the definition. They warned that the definition "restricts legitimate criticism of Israel and harms the fight against antisemitism."[7]

In thinking about words and their power, I realized some terms related to the Holocaust, including "the Holocaust," were untraceable in my memory. They seemed to exist as if I'd always known them, always been aware. Auschwitz, for example, was not a word I was taught outright, but one I implicitly understood, even at a young age. Auschwitz, the word for evil. Auschwitz, the name for death. I had no image for it, the name feeling more like a symbol than a place with real coordinates. The size, the layout, the history—I knew nothing of its details. And for most of my life, I was fine not knowing. I didn't want to see it clearly. Bubbie had been there when she was young and that felt like enough information. This is what I thought. Or what I thought I thought. But I had another memory, too.

Near the end of eighth grade, my class took a trip to Washington, D.C. We spent a full day at the United States Holocaust Memorial Museum, my first time at such an institution. I walked through the exhibition rooms, dark and winding, looking for Bubbie's name on every plaque in the building. I looked for her face too, in all the pictures on all the walls, but I knew I'd never know it even if I did spot it. The youngest photo I'd seen of Bubbie was from her wedding day. I craved some recognition of her life, of the truth I felt but did not know. In the museum's Hall of Remembrance, I lit a candle with black and white images of other people in my head. I left the museum feeling empty, like I'd been hollowed out, scooped clean. Later I asked Bubbie if she'd ever been to a Holocaust museum before and she scoffed, "I can't stand those places." It surprised me at the time, but I understood. The museums commemorated the thing she most wanted to forget. They were not designed with her in mind.

After the trip, my social studies teacher assigned my class a family history project. He explained that we would have to interview a relative and write a report on their life. Right away I knew who I wanted to call.

Bubbie was a mystery to me. I couldn't imagine what her life had looked like before I'd become a part of it. All I knew was that when she was thirteen, the same age I was, she'd been in the Holocaust. I had no specifics on what that meant, just a sense that no one wanted to talk about it. No one ever did. I tried to picture my grandma as a thirteen-year-old girl—small? funny? athletic?—but came up blank. She seemed so set in her ways to me, an adult through and through. I called her that night.

"What do you want to know?" she said.

She seemed willing to talk. I pressed the kitchen phone to my ear and asked the only question I could think of. "What happened?"

She sighed.

Our phone call was short, twenty minutes at most. I was shy and awkward, unsure what to ask her, and she was antsy, uneasy around her own memories. She shared what she could with me and I wrote her answers down, line by line, careful to capture every word.

After I typed up my report, I printed it longways and bound the pages like a book. The cover was sky-blue construction paper, I remember that. What I don't remember is what I wrote. Not a word of it. Sometime after my teacher graded my report and gave it back to me, either that year or another, I lost it. I have no memory of what I said in it, the names and details I happened to save, remember, lose and forget. The past was slippery; forgetting, intentional or not, seemed to run in my family. Perhaps it wasn't that I didn't want to know, but that I didn't want to keep knowing. I didn't want the past around me, tugging on my sleeves, pulling me down. I learned from the rest of my family. Bury the past, ignore the pain. Bubbie forgot by busying herself in the kitchen. My mom, at work. I forgot by never really knowing in the first place, never asking too many questions, or never letting the answers fully settle when they did trickle in. In one way or another, we all tried to forget what had been lost. Maybe then it wouldn't feel like so much was missing.

This time around I wanted to do better. In the months before and after my trip, I submerged myself in Holocaust literature, determined to learn. It had been years since I'd last read about the war or studied it in school. (In that I was not unique. My mom once told me she'd tried to read *The Diary of A Young Girl* by Anne Frank several times, but could never make it through the whole thing, knowing how it ended. "But she doesn't write about that," I told her. "It doesn't go that far." "But I know," she said.)

Unsure where to start, I drifted in the direction I always drifted: to the library. I picked up several books, all written by survivors. With each page I read, I learned something new, felt something sharp inside. The details were horrific. Each account was distinct, shocking in its own way. These survivors' recordkeeping, their capacity for language, specificity, and grace, all amazed me. How much did Bubbie recall? How clear were her memories?

Cracking open a notebook, I created a list of questions to ask her. They covered nearly every year of her life.

It was more than curiosity driving me. As I wrote out my questions, an urgency to preserve her story came over me—now while she was living, now while she could remember. Her illiteracy ensured the details of the past would be lost otherwise. An old phrase of my parents echoed in my ears. "You know," they'd say to me, "we don't know how long your grandparents will be around," referring to both my dad's dad, my mom's mom and my own reluctance to talk on the phone as a kid. Though Bubbie seemed invincible to me, my parents were quick to remind me otherwise.

My notebook filled with interview questions. Auschwitz loomed large in my mind, the word ominous and immense. I wanted to know how it affected her, those first few days in the camp, the initial shock of it all. I wanted to know how it affected us, her family, so many years removed. There was so much I did not know or understand, so much I hadn't given thought to before. I was always forgetting to remember.

SEVEN

Of the camps Golda saw, none was more terrifying than Auschwitz. It was the largest of all the Nazi concentration camps, with more functioning gas chambers and crematoria than any other site. The camp complex, located in southern Poland, sat on fifteen square miles of isolated land—more than twice the size of downtown Philadelphia, about three times the size of the town I grew up in—and held three sub-camps: Auschwitz I; Auschwitz II, known as Auschwitz-Birkenau; and Auschwitz-Monowitz, or Buna. The Nazis began construction of the camp in April 1940 and received the first transport of prisoners in June of that same year.

Upon the front gate of the camp, large wrought iron letters formed an archway, declaring to all who entered *Arbeit Macht Frei*. In English, this translates to *Work Sets You Free*. It proved to be a cold irony. In 1941, the SS—the Nazi paramilitary organization charged, among other things, with running the camps—tested poison gas as a means to commit mass murder at Auschwitz. After demonstrating its effectiveness as a lethal weapon—yes, poison gas does poison and kill—they developed a plan to scale its usage, tripling the number of facilities with dedicated gas chambers in short order. Death counts soared at the camp and new transports—men, women and children pulled from cities and villages, big and small, all across Europe—started arriving on a near-daily basis. The vast majority were Jews, but deportees also included Roma and Sinti people, homosexuals, disabled people, political opponents of the Nazis, Jehovah's Witnesses, non-Jewish Poles, and more. The United States Holocaust Memorial Museum estimates that, in total, the SS and police deported "at least 1.3 million people to the Auschwitz complex between 1940 and 1945. Of these, the camp authorities murdered approximately 1.1 million."[8]

Selection began as soon as the doors of the train cars flung open. The SS yelled at the people disembarking, dividing the men from the women. Like that, nearly every family was cleaved in two. The women almost always took the children. Next, SS doctors examined each person. These officials looked for what they considered good age—older than fourteen, but younger than sixty—and good health, too. The SS wanted their slave laborers to be strong, able-bodied individuals. Those deemed fit for hard labor were sent to the right side and organized in lines of five, many rows deep, like an army. In this way the SS could count and control their new state prisoners.

To the left side, the SS cast the elderly. They were considered too feeble for the manual labor demanded by the Nazis. Children were also sent to the left, deemed unfit for work of any kind. Their mothers, otherwise strong and healthy women, accompanied them. Old, young, or moms, they were all sent to the gas chambers. Once the gas had taken their lives, their naked bodies were pillaged for gold teeth and other valuables, then burnt to ashes. Tall brick chimneys pushed the smell up and out, choking the sky. It was a smell no living prisoner could ignore.

Though not the architect of this system, Dr. Josef Mengele became the most infamous Nazi at Auschwitz. He was often found on the incoming train platform, evaluating new prisoners whether he was on duty or not. As he eyed the lines of people, he not only looked for signs of health and age, but also for potential test subjects. Dr. Mengele, or the "Angel of Death" as his prisoners dubbed him, conducted inhumane pseudo-medical experiments on the people of the camp. His tests included placing his subjects in pressure chambers, burning them with phosphorous, submerging them in water for hours on end, injecting them with malaria and spotted fever virus, infecting their wounds with mustard gas, lacing their food with poison, sterilizing and castrating them, conducting gruesome autopsies on those who died—which a majority did—and afterwards, collecting their eyes to mount on a wall in his lab. He had a particular obsession with twins, especially young child twins, who he saw as valid control variables for his many experiments. In the winter of 1943, Dr. Mengele was granted a promotion to Chief Camp Physician of Auschwitz II. His new title gave him authority to do as he pleased in the camp. He could select, torture, dismember, maim or kill any prisoners he'd like, in any manner he so desired.

Golda Indig was shipped to Auschwitz-Birkenau with her family in the spring of 1944, several months after Dr. Mengele's promotion. She was a scared thirteen-year-old girl with no knowledge of where she had been taken or what was about to happen. (There were several parts of her story that she would later gloss over unless asked directly, and often even then. They were too painful for her to recall, memories too heavy to hold. One of these incidents involved a female SS guard at Auschwitz clubbing Golda in the head. She never mentioned this when talking about the camp, only later when reflecting on the injury, on the medical care she had to seek after the war. Only then did it feel safe to remember. Another agonizing memory, perhaps the most difficult part of her story to get through, was the first selection, her first minutes inside the gates of Auschwitz. It was a place she could not linger; a spot, even in memory, she could not bear to be.)

After three days on the train, Golda stepped out of the rancid darkness and into the camp. The light was sudden and harsh. Immediately she was separated from her brother Mechel. It happened in a single blink, a frightening and chaotic blur of a moment. There were no goodbyes. Men were yelling at them, dogs barking. Golda was left with her mom Henia, her older sister Blimchu and her two younger siblings Meilekh and Rojha Blima, all huddled together. Like that, the six became five.

Golda's mom saw what was happening around them and understood. There was no way out. She took off her thick fur coat and wrapped it around Golda's slender shoulders, hoping it'd make her daughter look a little older, a little more mature. It was all she had left to give. Henia pulled her two eldest girls in close. Stick together, she told them. Without a word more, she and the two younger ones were pushed to the left side and ushered swiftly to their deaths.

From five to two. The elder sisters clung to each other.

Wearing her mom's heavy winter coat, Golda waited for her first SS examination. Her sister Blimchu, the older and taller of the two, went first. She stood in front of the SS guard and he looked her up and down, pointing to the right. Golda followed her sister's example, standing in front of the guard in her mom's coat, trying to look as strong and mature as she could. The guard looked at her and pointed to the right. She passed.

The sisters were placed in a group of women and forced to shower and discard their clothes, the only remaining items they had from home. All they were given in return was a single grey shift dress.

The SS guards weren't done. After taking the girls' clothing, they shaved their heads. Hair was of great value to the Nazis since they had found ways to spin it into hair-yarn and make industrial felt from its coarse strands, both of which could be put to use in military and commercial endeavors. The Nazis manufactured army blankets with human hair and turned the locks of their prisoners into thick socks for the feet of U-boat crewmen. Private German companies used the hair to make other textiles. Because girls like Golda and Blimchu wore their hair long, longer than most of the Nazis' male prisoners, their tresses were considered especially useful.

When Bubbie recalled her time in Auschwitz to me, she made sure to mention the coffee. It had a harsh bitter taste, unlike anything she'd had to drink before. With so many female prisoners no longer getting their periods, a rumor spread through the camp that the coffee was tainted. They all talked about it. The women feared the coffee was changing their bodies, ending their menstrual cycles, possibly even sterilizing them. Researchers have investigated these claims and found no evidence of a Nazi program to halt menstruation through chemical additives. What is far more likely is that the women stopped getting their periods because they stopped getting nutrition, starvation being the ultimate culprit. And the coffee? It was just bad.

After several weeks in the camp, Golda and Blimchu were rounded up for another selection. There was going to be a second, more thorough examination. The girls' palms sweated helplessly, their stomachs too empty to growl. Golda no longer had her nice shoes, her mom's fur coat or her own dark brown locks to help her look a little older. Everything had been taken from her. Everyone was gone except for Blimchu, who now stood in line beside her for the next selection. By this point, the sisters understood what it meant not to be selected for work.

Blimchu went first. The SS guard looked her up and down, examining her body, health, age and height. At the guard's side was a mean-looking dog, a German shepherd with sharp teeth. The officer took one more glance and pointed to the right. Blimchu was safe, at least for the moment. She was sent to the line for work. At seventeen, she was strong and fit, in good shape despite the deprivation.

Next, it was Golda's turn. Her family had never been wealthy, but she had always had something to eat and clothes to keep her warm. Now, she had neither. The SS guard stared at her thirteen-year-old body. The lack of food at the camp had weakened her and made her muscles look sickly and slight, too slight for physical labor. The guard didn't hesitate. He pointed to the left.

From two to one.

Golda did as she was ordered and walked over to the left side. For the first time, she found herself separated from her entire family. She stood amongst the weakest prisoners, the most emaciated, ribcages pressing through skin. She could no longer squeeze her sister's hand or look to her for comfort. She couldn't see her at all. In a mass of starving strangers, Golda was alone. She was standing in the line to die.

EIGHT

— All of a sudden, they say, *I have a group and they go in the other building*. Neighbor building, you know? OK. So me and my sister, we go back there in the neighbor building and from there, they picked out people to go to work. One by one, everybody went and say nothing. We had to go.

Finally, again they examine people who going: right, left, right, left. I was the youngest, the skinniest. They pushed me to the left to be burned.

The rest of the group, they went back. And we had to wait in line till the rest of them finish looking over. And looking over, it takes time. The other group where I was before that, she came by. She saw me in the left lane. She waved to me, *Come in my lane*. She went, *Walk close by the other lane so you can sneak in*. And I went back to my sister in the other lane. That's how once I didn't end up to be burned. One time.

— Was that the Polish lady? Who said your family was burning?

— The Polish lady was watching us. The Polish people, they were six years in there. Some of them, they put to work to watch us. She was helping me.

So, they had the whole group looked over. Then we had to march on the other side of the building, they had showers, big building with showers. We went there, in the backyard. We were still lining up.

There was Mengele with another soldier, looking us over. *Go, go, one by one, go.* Look us over, up and down. We have to do what they say. *Quiet. Line up. Go. You go to work, you go here.*

Again, they pushed me to the left side to go to crematorium. Again.

There was a few people there. Luckily, somebody looked away, I run behind the big building. I don't know how I got the guts. Sneaked away, I went all the way to the other end of the building where the other line of people was to go to work. And my sister was crying, *Oh my gosh, my sister, my sister, my sister.* Finally I get to the end of the building. And I said, *Oh my gosh, I have to sneak to the other side. What am I going to do?* I'm thinking. Finally, one SS woman, another SS woman, meet on the street and they start talking. They found each other and they talking. And I run in the group who went to work, you know, and they kept pushing me back. *We already five, go, go, go. Go away from here, we already five in the line.* They kept pushing me and pushing me, all the way to the end. Finally I can stop. There was four, I was the fifth. And my sister, she saw me there. I pinched her to be quiet. *I am also here.*

NINE

The morning after our first interview, I went to the ocean. Bubbie's building was a ten-minute walk from the shore. She was asleep, but I was up and eager to get some air. The weight of the previous night's conversation hung over me. I'd thought I already knew her story, already knew what happened all those years ago in Germany and Poland. But it turned out I was wrong. The pieces I knew were a sliver of the horror she had faced and the nerve she had faced it with. It stunned me, the depth of her pain and courage. The intensity of it, how raw it all still was for her. The close calls, the selections, one after another, being only thirteen in a barbed-wire death camp in a foreign country—I couldn't hold it all in my head. I grabbed Bubbie's keys from the kitchen counter and inched my way out of the condo as quietly as I could.

The beach was nearly empty, a rare sight. Only a few shirtless old men dotted the view. I slid off my sandals, walking north along the water, away from the silver-backed waders. Lost in thought, pieces of Bubbie's story returned to me, knocking about my foggy head. The smell of salt swirled in the air around.

I pictured her and her sister being packed into a grimy room like herring. One by one, squeezed into barracks like lifeless fish. I thought about how she had shouted when she said this—*herring!*—and how I had never had herring before, not even as a kid, choosing instead between Fruit by the Foot, Gushers or Koala Yummies. I thought about the bowl of food every six people shared, sitting on the grimy floor. Where had it come from? Who served it? Were there no spoons at Auschwitz or did the guards withhold them? I thought about the Polish lady at the camp, whose name I will never know, and how she pointed at black columns of smoke and screamed at my grandma and her sister. *Your family is burning there!* What a horrible thing to bark at a child. Clearly, her words haunted Bubbie: a taunt told with truth, a cage, a lock.

> *Your family is burning there!*
> *Your family is burning there!*

I kept walking, my toes carving dark lines behind me as I dragged them through the damp sand.

The Polish lady was a Kapo at the camp, a fellow prisoner in charge of supervising and commanding the group. Kapos received certain privileges over other inmates. Desperate to stay in good graces with their Nazi tormentors, they were often vicious to those beneath them. The Polish lady was no exception. And yet, when she found Bubbie in the line for the gas chamber, the line to die, she risked her own life to pull her out. Later, when Bubbie was placed back in that same doomed line, it was this act of courage from the Kapo that gave her the idea to escape on her own. The woman terrified her and also saved her life. She hardened her and her sister to the realities of Auschwitz and put the keys to survival, or the keys to possible survival as no survival was ever certain or complete, into the palms of their young hands. Bubbie was barely a teenager. Already her life had been saved three times: first by her mother, then by the Kapo, then by her own two feet.

Several yards off the coastline, a patch of baby palm trees rustled in the breeze. They were tiny, as cute as trees can be, with delicate fanned-out leaves and thin, wobbly trunks. A neon cord marked the lot, staked only a foot above the sand. I wondered how the little palms kept from being swept away in every high tide, every storm with a name. They barely reached above my knees.

I kept walking. What I was stuck on, what I could not stop thinking about, was the Polish lady. She was a blip in Bubbie's life; she was a monumental force. I wondered how old she had been when she was a Kapo at the camp, if she'd had any family with her in Auschwitz. Maybe a sister? An aunt? Mostly, I wondered what happened to her. Did she survive the brutality of the camps? Did she go on to have children and grand-children? Was she able to tell them her story from a penthouse apartment five blocks off the Atlantic Ocean? My feet sunk deeper into the sand, the waves batting at them, as I knew what the most likely answers were.

Before our interview the night before, Bubbie and I cleaned up our plates from dinner. A quietness came over us, a soft hum running through the room. There was a stillness we didn't want to disturb, but knew we had to. I opened the video app on my laptop while Bubbie sat in her armchair. How fidgety my hands were, trying to click the button. We sat side by side in the living room and began the interview. Only it wasn't so much an interview as a one-woman monologue. Bubbie spoke without prompting, coursing through her story, jumping from one unthinkable memory to the next. Before we'd started, I had assumed we'd have a casual conversation, an intimate exchange between grandmother and granddaughter, question and answer. I kept my notebook of interview questions close at hand. But Bubbie had other plans. For much of the conversation, she barely looked my way, speaking instead to the tiny black camera at the top of my laptop. At one point, she stared straight at the camera and introduced herself. "My name is Golda Indig..." she started, addressing someone who was clearly not me. I knew my grandma's name. For her, these conversations were the opposite of casual. They were official records, part of a greater human testimony. Part of history itself. And she was determined to get it right.

As Bubbie wound her way into the past, her voice changed shape and her composure wavered. She moved from raw distress to bitter anger to a kind of wretchedness I've never known. She adjusted the cover on the arm of her armchair again and again. It never seemed to sit right for her. She shouted in German, something I had never heard her do before. *Heraus!* she yelled, recalling the ire and disdain of an SS man. *Heraus! Heraus!* I had to look the word up later. It means out.

Bubbie had to relive the war in her head to tell me what happened. She re-heard the voices, loud and vicious, spittle on their statements, and saw the sunken faces of neighbors she had once known well. She re-felt the sting of cold against her arms and held herself, trying to stay warm despite the balmy Florida air outside. The trauma came back to her in clear and vivid waves while the words for it lagged behind, a permanent delay. Before processing the details of one sadness, another appeared before her, as vicious and cruel as the last. Her hands waved with feeling and she grew more animated as she spoke, the anger building. Her anger stunned me, so unlike her normal disposition. Bubbie mimicked soldiers and guards, other prisoners and survivors, her aunt, her sister, my grandfather. We were both in a trance of sorts, held captive by the horrors of the past, by the way her memories bled into each other, one after another after another. Pain, not chronology, linked them together. Time blurred, whole geographies melted in her hands. I sat back in awe. Sometimes, as she was telling her story, she'd say Detroit but mean Sighet, the present being more accessible than the past. Other times, the opposite was true. She got stuck in the distant past, lost perhaps, using the present tense for events that happened more than seventy years ago. Was that a slip of the tongue or the mind? She went so fast, I could never tell. I had no way to know if her slip-ups stemmed from her aging brain, the way her memory had become a sieve, or from the trauma itself. Was it a matter of too much time having passed? Or one of stress, a deep-rooted mental block? When she spoke of her wedding, for example, she told me her sister Blimchu was "here for it" as if the nuptials were last month or in this country, or as if I'd also been around and in attendance. She caught herself right away, telling me that I was not there for her wedding. I nodded. (Bubbie had been married in Eastern Europe in the late 1940s. But more on that later.)

I listened to her speak and asked questions where I could. I didn't have to ask too many questions—the trauma poured out of her in paragraphs—but also, I couldn't bring myself to ask too many questions. It felt like picking off someone else's scab and poking it until it bled. Until it gushed blood, until it oozed. She had never showed me this side of her before, the side that hurt. I couldn't bear to see her in so much distress.

Prying has never been my strong suit. Even if I am curious, even if I want to see what's cooking, I am not one to step forward and stir the pot. I am not so bold. The notebook I brought with me, full of questions for Bubbie, things I was eager to know, sat unopened on the couch. Semi-frozen, I watched in silence, my knees bent underneath me, my hands hot, knowing it was too late to go back now. The pot was stirring, bubbling over on its own accord.

I tried to clarify details as she spoke—who said that? where were you again? when was this?—but Bubbie was much faster than me. She flew through the most harrowing parts of her story, the ones I most wanted to hear, the way a stone skips over the surface of a pond. She never slowed to see the ripples, to reflect upon their impact. Sprinting through the camp, sneaking into her sister's work group, evading armed guards—she never dwelled on these actions, how close she'd been to death and danger. She couldn't. She had no space from her memories, from the fear and grief of the moment. She couldn't step back enough to examine or analyze, to reflect on the depth of her pain. Even after all these years, she was still too close to it. She was thirteen years old, eyes wide, a girl on the lookout for trouble.

The contrast between where we were—an air-conditioned living room in south Florida—and where she had been—an overcrowded death camp in Nazi Germany—felt as sharp as shears to me. She had come so far, done so much, to get here. So much struggling, so much scraping by. All I had done was not miss my flight. For years, I had known guilt as a passing remark from a relative, easy to brush off or ignore. It was a tactic to use, a way to suggest or insist, subtle and forceful all at once. I could see it a mile away, a biting comment in sheep's clothing. Now the concept transformed in front of me. The guilt was no longer someone else's sly retort, but a body with a gravitational pull all its own. It drew me in and did not let go.

For such a powerful, entangling feeling, it struck me as quite simple. Someone had survived something terrible and I was doing fine. Bubbie's hardships had nothing to do with me and yet there I was with my never-empty stomach, countless opportunities, and the ability to bend my life in whatever direction I so chose. She never had those options, but I always did. In high school, when all I wanted was to go to a college with a good communications school that was also far away, I applied to my top choice, a school that took two flights to get to, and I got in, enrolling as soon as the acceptance letter hit my family's mailbox. I had my pick of classes there, of professors and activities, clubs and jobs. My brother Scott came to visit me, my parents, several friends from home. I worried about what I'd do afterward and then, when afterward came, I worried about what I should wear to work, which bus I should take, what I should do for lunch. I worried about whether I'd be able to finish my library books before they were due, and if my running shoes would last through the rest of the summer. I worried about finger injuries from rock climbing and if all those hot-and-cold contrast baths were doing anything to help. I worried about the carrots in my fridge and when they might go bad. How long are carrots supposed to last anyway? Does it matter if they're baby carrots or full size, or if I forgot to wash them? I worried about the future and what I'd do with it, but much more so about the present, every detail of it, from when to set my alarm clock to where to tell a friend to look for parking to the best way to sign off a work email. Sincerely? Thank you? Best?

How frivolous it all felt now. Everything I had ever worried about felt small and petty in the face of Bubbie's oral history. I felt small and petty. What did any of it matter? A knot formed in my stomach. It seemed to clear its throat.

In this way, the ocean served as a lozenge for me, a break from the condo, a break from the narrative. The air at Bubbie's place had grown swamp-thick, heavy with the past, and I needed a change of scenery not to clear my mind, but to think it. There was so much processing to do. Thoughts, like sand, clung to me. As I walked back to her building, the wind peeled wisps of hair out from my ponytail. I tucked the loose strands behind my ears, where they stayed for half a second. It was clear: they were in the wind's hands now.

I tried to unlock Bubbie's door as silently as possible, but she was already up and opening it for me. I wasn't sure how she felt about me leaving earlier without saying anything—with anyone else I'd have left a note or sent a text—but she didn't seem to mind at all. She was not so watchful, not so quick to worry. If anything, it gave her time to make the two of us breakfast. She opened the door for me and shooed me to the table. The food was ready.

Every morning she whipped up something different for us to eat, but that first morning was potato latkes left over from the night before. They sat on a small plate, stacked one on top of another like an ancient edifice. Tufts of steam rose from the top. The edges were still sharp, a beautiful shade of dark golden brown. I breathed in the rich, warm smell.

In case the heaping plate of latkes wasn't enough, Bubbie brought out more. On the table in front of me appeared a full loaf of challah bread, a platter of breaded chicken, a bowl of cut fruit, a bag of crescent roll cookies and some cold, pulp-free orange juice. She took a seat across from me and I smiled at the spread. It was way too much food, a ridiculous amount. Only Bubbie would put out this much food for a two-person breakfast. There was no way we could eat it all, or even half of it. Not that that mattered. The eating is never the point. The feeding is. The filling. And so we picked up our forks and fed ourselves, gearing up for another full Florida day.

TEN

The SS marched Golda and Blimchu's new work group out of Auschwitz and onto a train. The girls didn't know where they were going, but they were glad to leave. Golda stayed close to her sister on the train, another pitch-black cattle car with nowhere to sit. They wondered how long the ride would take, where the tracks would take them, what kind of labor they'd be forced to do, and when they might get something to eat. Finally, the train stopped. The doors ripped open. The sisters stepped out of the train car and into a brush of woods. Tall pine trees surrounded them, an uncountable number. Their branches stretched up and out, casting vales of shadow below. From the train station, the SS marched the group along a paved road that cut through the dark, towering trees. The air was clean in a way it wasn't at Auschwitz. The group walked until buildings emerged in the distance: wooden barracks and watchtowers, a looming front gate, fencing that glinted with silver razor wire. They had arrived at the camp. But where were they?

After I sat with Bubbie, I knew more than I'd ever known before. I knew she had sprinted out of the line for the gas chamber and squeezed herself into her sister's work group. I knew the group was boarded onto another train, moved to a small forced labor camp hundreds of miles away. I knew Golda turned fourteen in this camp, hidden in a forest, far from home.

I did not know the name of the camp.

She said it, but I couldn't make it out, couldn't spell it. The name sounded like Heshnestadt. Or Kitchenstadt? It was a German word, and my grandma's pronunciation came with a heavy Hungarian accent. I wanted to get it right and so, back in my own apartment, I made a list of everything I knew:

> - *The name ended in –stadt.* That part I heard.
> - *Some prisoners, if not all, were women.*
> - *Some, if not all, came from Auschwitz.*
> - *There was a kitchen inside the camp where prisoners made soup.*
> - *There was a factory outside the camp where prisoners made munitions.*

That was it. That was all I knew. But how could I not know? How could I let this name, this piece of our history, slip away? I couldn't write about a place I couldn't name, a labor camp I couldn't locate.

I had no choice. I had to find it.

Online I stumbled on a list of major Nazi concentration camps during World War II. Only one name ended with -stadt. This seemed promising. Terezin, I read, was a ghetto-labor camp roughly forty miles outside Prague. It was also known as Theresienstadt. Could this be the camp?

Women were imprisoned at Theresienstadt. It had kitchens, too, although descriptions of fresh baked bread didn't quite match Bubbie's recollections of soup every night. Maybe she forgot? She often called me by my cousins' names until she could come up with mine, so it seemed possible.

But I kept discovering more: families managed to stay together at Theresienstadt? And there were soccer fields? The camp, I learned, served partly as a model ghetto for Nazi propaganda and partly as a holding pen until people could be moved (and for the most part, murdered) elsewhere. In the meantime, prisoners were allowed more of a cultural life there than at any other camp. There was a library at Theresienstadt, a school, even musical performances. I was fascinated, but confused. Where was the arms factory?

On YouTube, I found it.

In 2013, a man named Glen Emery filmed a series of motorcycle rides outside the camp, posting them to his channel Prague Moto Vlog. In one, Emery navigates a narrow road, passes a dog training center, parks his bike, grumbles about its weight, and hikes through a muddy forest until he reaches a large metal door in the side of a hill. There, on the screen of my laptop, shrouded by crumpled leaves and thick moss, was the entrance to the factory I'd been looking for. I stared at the rusted-over door. "What a horrible place, man," Emery says as he inches closer. "Zakaz vstupu, forbidden entrance. I'll say. Man, this a scary place."

Two miles outside of Theresienstadt, in a town called Litomerice, the Nazis turned an abandoned limestone mine into a military manufacturing site. Forced laborers excavated the stone, leaving behind a labyrinth of underground production halls. From a standard mine, they created three covert arms factories stretching nearly eighteen miles underneath the Czech Uplands.

So, Thereseinstadt? This must have been it. Still, something didn't sit right with me. I kept searching for that one definitive detail. What I found was that prisoners made parts for engines at Litomerice, not munitions. Many, if not all, were men. I had recorded my initial conversation with my grandma and played it back to hear her pronunciation. I felt even more uncertain. I could call and ask her to say it again, but there were only so many times I could ask. I didn't want to push her too far, remind her too much. As if she could forget.

Online I found another list. This one, from the United States Holocaust Memorial Museum (USHMM), didn't outline the major concentration camps, but gave them all, every ghetto, forced labor and death camp in Nazi Germany. Called the Encyclopedia of Camps and Ghettos, the list was broken into multiple volumes. Why not one, I wondered. Why does everything have to be so complicated? So difficult?

This was why: from 1933 to 1945, there were more than 44,000 camps and ghettos across Europe. The number sat in my stomach like gum. I looked at that comma, all those zeroes, and downloaded the two PDFs. My fingers went on autopilot: file-find s-t-a-d-t. In the first PDF, -stadt was found 922 times. In the second, 738 times. Theresienstadt, it turned out, did not stand alone.

I knew the soccer fields sounded wrong.

I read every mention of the word -stadt. I learned about the prisoners at Duderstadt, forced to produce 30- and 40mm shells near Hannover, and Kommando Köln-stadt, a group of Soviet prisoners ordered to clear rubble from Cologne, Germany. I learned about Deborah E. Lipstadt, a member of the Academic Committee of the US Holocaust Memorial Council who happened to have the letters s-t-a-d-t in her name.

But what I really learned was how much horror had been carried out. How much suffering people like (and not like) my grandma had endured. Starvation, separation, imprisonment, enslavement, typhus, torment, bullets, gas. I felt like finding a sled and pushing myself down a long, steep hill.

Back on the USHMM website, I discovered a way to request records on a particular Holocaust survivor. Priority went to family members. I filled out the form, then forgot all about it, assuming there'd be nothing. There had never been anything before. No one in my family had any documentation, any formal records.

Months later, I received an email.

A research team had run my request through the Arolsen Archives, an online database with documents on millions of victims of Nazi persecution. For the first time, I saw the ship manifest that marked my family's entry into North America. I saw the paperwork that made their passage possible, the stamps sealing their fate. I discovered inquiry cards from 1956, the first requests my family made for information and restitution. Golda Indig, one card said, was held at the following camps: Auschwitz, Kürzenstadt, Bergen-Belsen.

There it was.

I emailed the researchers back. What more can you tell me about Kürzenstadt?

They emailed me back. Nothing, it doesn't exist.

The research team looked through all their sources and found no camps, towns or regions in Europe with the name Kürzenstadt. As far as they could tell, the name existed in one place only: an inquiry card someone submitted on my grandma's behalf. In other words, the name came from someone like me, someone trying to figure out how to spell this damn thing.

Once I started laughing, it was hard to stop.

After several months, a name came to me. Not a name for the camp—I was still stupefied on that—but for a person. Someone who had been there, who knew. Blimchu Milsztein, the great-aunt I never met, the sister who endured the same threats and risks as my grandma Golda. She was no longer alive, having died when she was seventy-four and I was twelve, but I could still submit a request for her records. I crossed my fingers, waiting to hear, hoping for something to appear in my inbox. For months, I waited.

The email came on a Thursday. The sisters, it said, were at a women's-only labor camp in Krzystkowice, Poland. In German, the town was known as Christianstadt.

Compared to other concentration camps, Christianstadt was small, a speck in the history books. It was built late in the war and held a little more than a thousand prisoners, all of whom were Jewish women. They hailed from across Europe, including Austria, Czechoslovakia, Hungary, the Netherlands and Poland. (Bubbie was considered a Hungarian Jew during the war, but a Romanian one before and after. Perhaps this was why delineations and labels meant so little to her. They changed without warning or notice.) The more I read, the more details I found that matched Bubbie's memories. The prisoners were given one meal a day, a small bowl of soup. Even a story she told me about a pregnant prisoner was there in the historical record.

Upon the women's arrival at the camp, the SS lined them up and demanded that any and all pregnancies be reported. Whispers spread through the lines. No one was sure what to make of the edict. Several women stepped forward and were taken away; what happened to them next is still unknown. Most likely, they were sent back to Auschwitz and to their eventual ends. One pregnant woman, part of the same barracks as Golda and her sister, decided not to report. She had been so deprived of food and nutrition that she didn't show a hint of a bump. She hid her pregnancy with relative ease until, at nine months, she went into labor in the middle of the camp. The SS women in charge delayed the start of the workday so they could stay and watch. The woman laid herself down on the ground and delivered her own baby, clutching it to her chest. It was stillborn. "Thank god," my grandma remembers her crying in Hungarian as she rocked back and forth. "Thank god. They cannot take it away." The SS wrapped the baby in newspaper and buried it in the forest. They sent the woman to work duty the following morning as if nothing had happened.

Work took several forms at the camp. At first, the majority of prisoners were placed in a forest commando. They cut down trees and dug trenches to create a road and railway. Schoolgirls and homemakers months and years earlier, these women now felled trees and cut their branches, removed the stumps, lugged steel rails through the clearings, poured cement to make concrete blocks and laid down heavy railroad tracks. Another group, the sand commando, slung sand onto wagons in preparation for the building of a waste incinerator. But, in time, almost all of these prisoners were diverted away from outdoor construction work and into making bombs.

Dynamit AG Nobel, a German chemical company still in operation today, ran the munitions factory outside Christianstadt. They used prisoners to fill its production floors and conduct its most perilous tasks. For these women, the work was brutal, life-threatening in many cases. They were exposed to dangerous chemicals on a daily basis and without receiving any proper training or instruction. None of them had a background in chemistry, engineering or other related fields. They were unprepared for the intensive work of building bombs.

Every day began the same way. Before departing for the factory, the SS held a roll call. To punish the women, they made these roll calls last for hours, yelling at them, forcing them to stand outside and at attention no matter the weather or time of day. The SS then marched the women from the camp to the munitions factory, a three-mile trek through the forest. Once at the factory, the women filled and cleaned grenades with their bare hands, coming into regular contact with toxic substances. With little to no ventilation, the factory's floors filled with fumes and a stagnant, suffocating heat. The women worked in shifts of twelve hours and were granted few to no breaks. Many suffered from seizures, burns and poisoning. A lack of food and sleep made them even more susceptible to danger.

At the end of their work shifts, they walked the same three miles back to the camp, enduring another lengthy roll call upon arrival. Their feet ached from the walk—inflamed, festering and often beginning to blister and bleed. They used whatever scraps of fabric or paper they could find to wrap them up. Still, the pain was incessant. The hunger, too. For dinner, the prisoners were given a meager portion of soup. It was the only meal they received, that day and every other, and it was never enough. The broth was thin, almost entirely water, and held no meat or protein. After dinner, the prisoners retired to their barracks for the night, lying on hard wooden bunks stacked three high. Each woman had her own space, a nook with a straw mattress she did not have to share. These bunks would prove to be the prisoners' sole source of respite, a small boon to their wellbeing.

For Golda, going to the munitions factory was a major risk. She was, in fact, too weak for such arduous work. She had been forced to hammer rocks in her first few days at Auschwitz and knew she would never be able to keep up with the demand of daily physical labor. Her starved adolescent body couldn't take the exertion. Besides, her name wasn't on the official roll. The Nazis had no record of her existence at the camp, no record of her still existing at all. If she were to join the group going to the munitions factory and somehow get caught, she'd likely be executed on the spot.

So instead she hid inside the camp for months on end, under the Nazis' noses. She hid outside buildings, in the bathrooms, underneath furniture, behind supplies, wherever she could tuck herself away and go unnoticed. She went from thirteen years old to fourteen crouched in a ball. While the SS guards were shouting orders, making threats and running command on the march to the factory, Golda was hiding back at the camp. During inspections, when the SS probed the barracks for contraband, she fled the buildings altogether, hiding in the woods. Her sister tipped her off and told her when to go. Hours later, she returned as silently as possible. Every day she learned to be more and more invisible, a skill that saved her life on a daily—if not hourly—basis.

Only at night was Golda's isolation ever broken. She slept in a bunk with her sister Blimchu below her and one of her cousins off to the side. In fact, everyone in the barrack was from Sighet, neighbors from back home. The girls' aunt Suri was at the camp too, but assigned to a different barrack, so they were never able to see or talk to her. Instead, they kept each other company. In their starvation, the sisters thought in food, imagining what rich and luscious treats they'd make if only they were able. Lying in their bunks, Blimchu would suggest a dish and Golda would offer a side to complement, and back and forth they went, their imaginary table growing longer by the minute. They dreamed of a feast with succulent brisket and sweet lokshen kugel, soft and creamy egg noodles cooked until crisp on top. The girls saw themselves making challah breads, fluffy and golden brown, like the ones their brother Bumme used to bring home from the bakery not so long ago. They remembered their mom's dinners, the savory spices and meats calling to their stomachs. They remembered the crescent roll cookies they made with their grandma Malka, the way she strew flour across the table to keep their rolling pins from sticking. As the sisters drifted asleep in a forest far from home, they talked about little triangles of dough and the sugarcoated nuts they'd sprinkle inside, how the cookies would rise in the oven and the sweet smell that would fill the room. Sometimes, the rest of their barrack would join in, pitching their own fanciful dreams of making and eating a full meal of food. Escape was in the imagination alone.

One night, before climbing into bed, Golda noticed how swollen and bruised her sister's feet were from marching to the munitions factory in poor shoes. She offered to take her place on the factory floor the next day, so Blimchu could stay back and rest, let her wounds heal. Blimchu refused. It was too dangerous an idea, too reckless. As the older sister, she considered it her duty to heed their mother's order that they stick together, even if it meant doing the exact opposite. What their mom had meant, what she had really asked of them, was that they take care of each other, that they survive together. Marching to the factory every morning, leaving her little sister behind in the camp, was the best way for Blimchu to do so. As difficult as it was, she was determined to look out for Golda, trying in every way she could to shield her from the hardships that surrounded them. Golda looked for ways to do the same.

The next morning, like all the mornings before, the SS yelled for roll call and the sisters' barrack emptied out, the girls lining up in straight rows to be counted. Blimchu was in her usual spot in the line and Golda was in her usual spot, hiding somewhere else. In all the months she was at Christianstadt, Golda never saw the horrors of the munitions factory, never made the three-mile march to its clandestine location in the woods. She didn't pour explosive powder into small-shell hand grenades or suffer a seizure on the factory floor. She held onto her strength and energy through hiding and kept it much longer than she otherwise would have been able.

When I told Bubbie the name of the camp was Christianstadt, she replied, "Yeah." She had never had any doubt as to what she was saying. I, on the other hand, was still learning how to listen. I was still learning about the war, how it stayed with a person, with their body, how it became a memory. How the memory became a story. Or, as was often the case, how the memory became a silence, an object lost, an absence as present as anything else. In Florida, I sat with that absence for the first time, felt its presence, hovering, hanging, heavy as ocean air.

ELEVEN

— They put us on the train to go to work. From Auschwitz to Christianstadt. Christianstadt, they had factories and guns to make the parts. We got a place to stay and then they say come out to work. Of course, I was hiding, I was an extra from Auschwitz. They want to burn me. They all went, they got jobs to do something with the machine, for the gun, everybody had to work something. Steel, I don't know. Then they came home late at night. Every day they had to walk a long way, to go there and to come back. And they were going there every day, they were going there. Finally, I had nothing to do. I was always hiding.

One day I go to the kitchen. *Can I help you peel potatoes? Or carrots? Can I help you do something?*

OK. Go downstairs and help the girls to do the work.

So I did some of the work, I did with the girls. Potatoes, carrots, you know. They cooked there eintopf for the people when they come home from work. They get, everybody got a bowl of eintopf. Everything mixed up, carrots, potatoes, whatever they could, they put in there. Of course, they didn't get much to eat. Only one time a day we got. So they all ate that, then they went back to the room to sleep for the next day. I sneak back into my building where my sister was staying and my friends from my city, from Sighet. We were twelve people in one room, but each had one bed. Like a soldier bed, you know. From wood. Piece of dirt. So I had a piece on top. I was going one step, two step, three—two step. And I was up there, upstairs. My sister worked, my cousin worked, my friends worked who's adult, you know. Everybody from my room but me. I had to keep on hiding whenever they came to inspect. One time I hide in the toilet. One time I hide in the…back, between the bags, you know, outside. When they tell them to go, I was hiding in the toilet or under the bed, somewhere. And what happened? They went by and said, *OK. Everybody clean, everybody nice. Keep doing what you're doing, working in the camp, in the Munitionsfabrik, in the factory.* Everybody was working, no you get nothing. Just try to work, and you cannot talk, you can't say nothing. Unbelievable.

What happened? Day after day, day after day, they doing that. The people, they went to work. Finally I had a chance to work in the kitchen. I used to sneak away a carrot, a potato. Stick it under my pants. And I go home and wait for them to come home for work. Of course they were scared. *What happens when they come?* I said, *Don't worry, I will hide it, don't worry.* Of course, I was skinny and tiny, my hair started to grow. All they can see is my big brown eyes, always running around, being cheerful, not being scared.

— You were cheerful?

— Hmm?

— You were cheerful? You weren't scared?

— No, when I was here, when they came home from work, no I wasn't scared. Still they went, they were there, going out, they had to go and what they do. After that I was OK… It was terrifying, terrifying.

TWELVE

In one of the many photo albums lying around Bubbie's condo, I found a picture of the two of us I hadn't seen in years. In it, I am two or three years old, standing on a chair in my family's old kitchen in Michigan. I slid the photo out of the album's plastic covering to get a better look. The sun glared through the balcony door and I burrowed myself into the couch to see.

The photo shows me beaming at the camera, a kid-sized apron around my neck and waist, a miniature rolling pin by my hands. Bubbie's eyes are turned toward the camera too, but her hands are moving in the opposite direction, reaching for an electric mixer, unable to pause. I had no memory of this particular moment, but seeing the photo reminded me of baking with her when I was a little older, when she took the train to Chicago to visit us and unloaded half her luggage straight into our fridge. Right away, she was in our kitchen, washing her hands, setting out ingredients. I remember it well. I was ten years old and knelt on a kitchen stool to watch.

Bubbie turned to the fridge and pulled out a ball of dough like a magic trick. I leaned over the edge of the countertop, as eager as ever, to see her spread handfuls of flour across the counters my parents worked so hard to keep clean. She flattened the dough with a rolling pin, stretching it a little further on every pass. As she worked the dough, she slowly lost my attention and the flour slowly gained it. I reveled in the mess of it all, the stacks of bowls and baking sheets, the streaks of white on my hands and face. With a finger, I doodled in the silky soft powder, drawing loops and swirls. Bubbie gave me excess dough to play with and I rolled, pinched and squished it like clay. I wanted to eat it too—it smelled amazing, as butter always does—and she let me, something my mom definitely would've said no to had Bubbie asked. But Bubbie never asked and I always got a few bites of delicious raw pastry dough.

Bubbie was a phenomenal cook. Instinctively, she mixed, kneaded, rolled, and baked. She used no recipe books, no precise measurements or amounts. Everything she knew was stored in her head and hands. She eyed each scoop of flour and dash of spice. She listened for the sound of sizzling oil and waited for the just-right smell of roasted goodness. She remembered every step, all the timings and temperatures. Memory is critical for the illiterate cook. There is no double-checking the cookbook, re-reading the recipe or writing your own notes for next time. You either remember, or you don't. And Bubbie remembered.

By the time I was kneeling on a stool to watch her, she had spent decades mastering her recipes. She held a massive bank of them in her head and could whip up a meal on a moment's notice. She made a mean matzoh ball soup, tender and succulent cholent brisket, and mouth-watering roasted chicken, which she served with potatoes, onions and carrots. She let the vegetables bask in the chicken's fatty juices, getting plump with flavor as they baked together in the oven. Her latkes were canon in my family: light, never oily; crisp, never limp; and always perfectly seasoned with onion and pepper. The interior, soft and savory, balanced the crunch of the exterior, a rich golden brown, salty and hot. The smell could reach every corner of every room.

Bubbie was always the last one to sit down and eat, running in and out of the kitchen, prepping one dish, pulling another. Her meals were plentiful, an endless amount of flavor for us to fill ourselves on. For dessert, she made pastries, sweets filled with nuts, cheese, chocolate or cream, finely shaped and baked, and always made in bulk. Though some of her dishes didn't appeal to my tame American taste buds, most hit me right in the belly. Creamy, fatty flavors, well-salted, buttered up—it was easy to get lost in all the smells coming out of the kitchen. They were from another world.

Once Bubbie had the pastry dough thin enough, there were two possibilities: she could make it into crescent rolls, a sweet and buttery cookie, or she could make a dessert we called creamish. Creamish was a family recipe, in that no other family I knew ever had it in their houses. It involved cold custard being neatly sandwiched between two crisp layers of pastry. I watched as Bubbie rolled the dough into a long sheet and lifted it onto a baking tray. With a butter knife, she trimmed its edges to make a perfect rectangle. Creamish then, I thought. We were making creamish.

Bubbie handed me a fork and told me to dot the dough. She explained: the dough would rise and bubble and crack if we didn't vent it first. This was important. I poked at it gently with the fork and she nudged me to keep going. More, more. She took the fork from me and demonstrated, stabbing lines of four holes all over.

The sheets of dough baked and cooled. In the process, more magic: the pastry sheets were now delicate and flaky, brittle enough to snap in half. Bubbie scooped cold vanilla custard onto one of the pastry sheets and with the back of a spoon, coaxed it into an even layer. She then laid the second sheet of pastry on top to match, careful not to let it crumble. To finish the dish off, she filled a metal sifter with powdered sugar. I tapped its side, sprinkling a flurry of white snow over the dish. More, Bubbie said. I added more and she said no, more. More, more. More.

More is my grandma's north star. It's her everything. She's seen what less looks like—less family, less home, less safety, less hair. The war gave her less of everything. What she wanted now was a fridge brimming with more: more soups with more hunks of meat; whole chickens simmering in fat; giant platters of golden pastries; greasy, crisp potato latkes; more cheese-stuffed blintzes; more jars of pickles and horseradish, eaten and emptied to hold more food; loaves of deeply browned challah bread; more matzah balls, fat and round; more cookies packed in gallon-sized plastic bags; and creamish, an avalanche's worth of powdered sugar on top, glimmering in that brilliant light, on as soon as you opened the refrigerator door.

Was it fear or defiance or pride that caused Bubbie's waist to expand in the years after the war? Was it grief or guilt that kept it that way? She went from a twig-like teenager to a buxom young woman, and from a buxom woman to an overweight one. Food became a haven for her, a distraction from everything else. The latkes, she found, never held grudges. The pans said nothing, and the soup didn't care. She cooked because she had to, because it was five o'clock, because someone was hungry, because it was easy for her, because so little was easy for her. She cooked because she missed her mom and grandma, because she liked having company over, because she couldn't sit still, because it gave her hands something to do, because she craved a sense of control, because fullness is elusive. Was that why she made so much food? Why the concept of portions never reached her ears?

It was not uncommon for Holocaust survivors to have food-related anxieties and health issues. In one study, researchers found that survivors were likely to store excess food and had difficulty throwing it away, even after the food had spoiled.[9] No doubt this was the case for Bubbie. Food was powerful, an essential fuel for the body, and she refused to let any of it go. She had once served me chicken soup that tasted like pickles because the jar hadn't been properly washed out and there was no going back. When she wasn't looking, I poured the sour broth down the sink.

Another study, conducted at the Icahn School of Medicine at Mount Sinai, found that Holocaust survivors had lower levels of cortisol, the body's main stress hormone.[10] Cortisol serves as a natural alarm system for the body, altering immune responses, controlling blood pressure, and increasing metabolism. Bubbie's alarm system was, in effect, turned off. Interestingly, the study also found that survivors had low levels of an enzyme that breaks down cortisol, helping them preserve the cortisol they did have and maximize stores of glucose, "an optimal response to prolonged starvation and other threats."[11] There was no question that Bubbie's wartime experiences still lived in her body, still wreaked their havoc. It was out of her control.

A study from Israeli and Canadian researchers showed that Holocaust survivors, when compared to peers born outside of Europe, had higher rates of obesity, hypertension, cancer and more—but also tended to live longer lives.[12] Bubbie's pill box was as full as her days and after every contradiction I read about in the research, came a nod, uncontrollable, from my head.

Like Bubbie, I couldn't stand throwing food away. Leaving something uneaten on my plate felt wasteful, sliding it into the trash even worse. When I went to the grocery store, I only bought food for a few meals. I rarely bought enough. As she was piling more onto her plate, I was piling less. To me, food was too precious to waste. I enjoyed it, the layers of flavor, the rising smells, the sauces and spices, but I only needed so much. In my apartment in Philly, my fridge was often half-bare. I didn't have Bubbie's capacity to hold onto food, to endlessly make more, to cook and cook and cook and cook.

In the years after the war, Bubbie turned a simple need into a fierce love. She cooked with that love, sampled from it, served it to others, and saved it for later. Food was the center of my family's universe, the point around which we all revolved. It was how we greeted one another, how we said congrats and I love you and I'm sorry. Whenever Scott and I visited Bubbie in Florida, she always had something ready for us to eat upon on arrival. "Come," she'd say, "Sit, sit!" She would retreat to the kitchen, re-emerging a second or two later with a warm meal made especially for us. She'd tell us to eat and like good grandchildren, we would. If a bite or two was left sitting on a plate afterward, she told one of us to have it. "Eat!" She could be quite pushy. If three or four bites were left, she ate them herself. For larger leftovers, she wrapped the food in plastic and put it in the fridge to serve the following day. Nothing was ever wasted. A year of starvation would not allow for that.

Once the creamish was ready, we ate it right away. Depending on who was cutting, a slice could be any size. A sliver, if my mom cut it. A square, if it was my dad. Scott always halved the last piece so he wouldn't have to clean the dish. This time it was Bubbie cutting. She gave me an envelope-sized rectangle of a slice. I slid my fork through it and took a careful bite. It was smooth and creamy, the custard oozing between my teeth, with a bit of crunch from the dough. The taste of powdered sugar clung to the corners of my mouth.

In recalling her creamish, a dessert Bubbie made on a regular basis, I realized I had never seen it in any menu or cookbook. I had never seen the name in print at all. The letters on the page looked odd to me, as if they were only meant to exist out loud, in the airspace of Bubbie's kitchen. This never mattered before, but now in writing, I was confronted with how much I didn't know. I figured *creamish* was probably not right, but my mom's suggested spelling of *creamage* felt even worse to me. Something so delicious should not appear so unappetizing in print. I started poking around online, trying to find the name of the dessert, coming up empty time and time again. It took me months of research, and years of baking with Bubbie, until I uncovered the correct spelling for the dish. In other places, it's called napoleon, kremówka, krempita, or cremeschnitte. In my grandma's corner of the world, it's krémes, the Hungarian word for creamy. No wonder my search queries kept coming up empty. There was no English version of the word. Hungarian custard slice, one site suggested. Honey cream layer cake, another insisted. None felt right. And so, I chose to stick with my original spelling. Creamish: light, playful, wrong, and ours. That was part of what Bubbie liked about cooking in the kitchen, and taught me to like about it too. There was always room for discovery, for invention and exploration and error and revision. The kitchen was a creative space. We were there to make. Make dough, make mistakes, make better, make more. Creamish was for eating, not spelling.

I laid the photo of the two of us on the coffee table and snapped a picture, so I could look at it later on my phone. I couldn't wrap my head around how she'd done it, how she'd mastered so many dishes and memorized so many measurements and steps. She learned to flip and turn with a single fork, never bothering with spatulas or other kitchen tools. She didn't need them. She perfected the combination of creamy custard, flaky pastry, and an easily distracted granddaughter. She embraced the glory and gluttony of more, its heavy consequences. She made dish after dish, feeding everyone who walked in (or by) her door, dinner and dessert. She brought us all together, brought us back, again and again, everyone gathered around the same dining room table. Everyone hungry and asking for more. I didn't know how she did it. I only knew that food was power, and Bubbie liked to make a lot of it.

THIRTEEN

— After nine months, they said, OK, line up. We're going back. We're going back in the building and from there we gonna go to Bergen-Belsen. We gonna walk six weeks to Bergen-Belsen.

Walking, we barely had clothes, barely had shoes. Every day we're walking, walking. No place to go lay down or rest. And it beginning to get dark, we dropped on the floor. It was snow, it was dirt here. We was trying to sleep a little, resting. That's what we did. I was laying on the snow and my sister, wherever you could. Snow wasn't that bad, some places was worse. The dirt. And we walked and we walked. Got up and walking again. Keep on walking. Very seldom that a German felt sorry for us. He said, *Come in my backyard, I have the cows, the horses, I send them away and you go in that room.* What they call it? Like where they keep the car you know.

— A barn.

— A barn. There was hay there and everything. After a couple hours, they bring a big pot with boiled potatoes. Oh we were so happy. Something to eat. Can you believe it? How happy we were. Finally, it got daylight again, they said, *Everybody out, out, line up, line up and keep on going.* We went, kept on going. Go, go, go. Before we get to Bergen-Belsen, people from upstairs, they saw us walking, hungry, barely making it. They threw bread down from the upstairs, from the window. And whoever picked it up, the SS shot, shot the people. Can't say nothing. *Leave the dead there. Keep on going. Go.* They holler, *Go. Go.* Unbelievable. Kept on going and going.

Six weeks walking, we didn't have shoes. Clothes, hardly any left. Kept on going, going, going. Finally we reach Bergen-Belsen.

Bergen-Belsen was like a big camp and the area where they put us down, on the floor, everybody lay down one by one. It take days and days, they don't give us a piece of bread, nothing to drink. I mean, you couldn't go in the bathroom anyway. We were laying on the floor, me, my sister, my aunt. And on this side was a lady with four daughters. From Sighet, that I know them. And laying there, nothing to eat, nothing to drink.

Day by day, we hear the bombs coming. Shooting at this and that. Liberation. Everybody hollered, *I wish they come here. And that they drop the bomb on us!* Everybody wanted to be dead already, finished, nothing to live for, the way they treating us.

We had nothing to do. Just lay there, waiting, waiting, the bomb to come. They didn't give us food or anything. And the lady next to me, one daughter died one day. The next day, another one died. And they threw them in a pile in the middle of the camp. And she cries and cries. Everybody has to worry about their bed, *What's going to be next to me? What is happening now?* She had four daughters. Only one left. And she died too, the mother. The one who's left is a young girl like me. Everybody else died. Dead, dead. Nice home, from Sighet. Unbelievable. Everybody dying, next to me. The right side, the left side.

Finally, they brought us a piece of bread, it so moldy. *Eat! If not you die also. Eat!* What can we do? We ate it. Nothing to drink. We were in such a bad shape.

One day went by, another day went by. We hear the bombs, we hear the noise of the airplanes coming and going. What happens? We gonna be liberated? What's going on?

FOURTEEN

As Allied forces advanced into German territory, the SS started relocating prisoners closer to the interior of the Reich. The leaders of the SS were adamant about not giving up any concentration camp prisoners. They were too valuable. Prisoners served as the main form of labor for German arms manufacturing. If the war turned back in Germany's favor, the Nazis would need as many prisoners as possible to ramp up military weapons production. If the war failed to turn in their favor, which seemed far more likely, some SS leaders believed they could use camp prisoners as hostages or bargaining chips in negotiations with the Allied powers. (They would be quite wrong in this assumption.) But perhaps more pressing than these reasons was the fact that prisoners were the only people who knew in depth, in granular and gruesome detail, what was happening behind the closed doors of the camps. The Nazis were desperate to keep them from sharing their stories of suffering and torment with the world. The truth was not something they would be able to recover from. So when advancing forces started closing in on the camps, the SS started evacuating every last prisoner inside. Everyone had to go.

At first, the SS moved people by train as they had always done before. It was the fastest and most efficient way to transport groups of people. However, as Allied and Russian forces improved their positions in the sky and on land, transport by train became near impossible for the Nazis. In addition to destroying arms factories, the Allies had bombed many vital German railway routes, too many to fix, at least right away. The SS was forced to rethink their plans.

Rather than halt camp evacuations, the Nazis decided to carry them out on foot. Covering broad swathes of Europe, these marches took weeks to complete, sometimes months. Most took place during winter, amidst vicious winds and icy snow banks. Prisoners were underfed and underdressed for the journey, already in weakened states from the starvation and forced labor they had endured at the camps. They looked like walking skeletons. Many of these prisoners collapsed from fatigue along the way, sapped from so many hours and days and weeks of walking in the dead of winter. When they fell, the SS shot them on the spot, killing them instantly. The intent was clear: no one was to escape alive.

Throughout the winter of 1945, approximately 250,000 prisoners died from exhaustion, starvation, murder, and exposure as evacuations by foot continued.[13] Today, they are known as the death marches.

(It's worth noting that people did escape during these marches, including several from the march from Christianstadt to Bergen-Belsen. Ruth Kluger, one of these survivors, writes in her book *Still Alive*, "We six turned on our heels and ran down the street…We were free—free to be hunted down if our luck should turn. But I remember the exuberance, the euphoria of these moments."[14] Reading her words, knowing what would have come had they stayed, I feel euphoria too.)

Many of the death marches were headed for Bergen-Belsen, a concentration camp in northwest Germany, far from the front lines of war. The camp had been designed to hold 10,000 prisoners, but the sudden evacuations of other camps caused the population to balloon. By the end of 1944, more than 15,000 prisoners were at Bergen-Belsen. Four months later, the number had quadrupled. Nearly 60,000 people were being held in the confines of the camp in April 1945. Among some of the later arrivals were Golda and her sister Blimchu. They had traveled by foot and boxcar, covering more than 280 miles to get there.

The overcrowding at Bergen-Belsen was disastrous. Prisoners went days without receiving anything to eat or drink, leading to mass starvation and malnourishment. When they were given food, it was often stale or covered with mold. The camp's already poor sanitary conditions worsened. Soon enough, the complex became disease-ridden. Outbreaks of illness spread throughout the camp including typhus, tuberculosis, typhoid fever and dysentery. The worst of the epidemic was typhus, which came with high fevers, purple rash, severe muscle pain, nausea and vomiting. Those afflicted with the disease were often found in a stupor, deeply fatigued and disoriented to their surroundings. Where before there were the dead and the living, now there were the dead and the dying. Everyone was suffering and in immense pain. Typhus took the lives of thousands of people at Bergen-Belsen including, most famously, Anne Frank and her sister Margot, who were buried in one of the mass graves at the camp. They were nearly the same ages as Golda and Blimchu, but from the other side of the continent.

On April 15, 1945, Bergen-Belsen was liberated. The Nazis, not wanting to face a potential disease outbreak from the camp with fighting happening so close nearby, offered to turn Bergen-Belsen over to British forces. They signed a deal with the 11th Armoured Division of the British Army for a peaceable surrender of the camp, the only concentration camp to be formally released to the Allies. British troops walked in days later. When Bubbie told me the story, she called the liberators Americans or even, The American. These were the rumors running through the camp at the time, whispers that spread from person to person. I have to imagine that a Brit and an American looked awfully similar to a famished fourteen year-old who had never seen either one before. Years later, this was probably still the case. (I told Bubbie that it was the British and not the Americans who liberated the camp, and she replied, "Oh. OK.")

When the British strode into Bergen-Belsen, they were horrified by what they saw. Corpses lay in heaps, one on top of another like worn clothes. The bodies had turned yellow, the skin stretched and slick with nothing more than bones underneath. Those who were still alive existed amidst the piles of dead—moving, eating, and sleeping in close quarters to the departed. They had nowhere else to go. Besides, many of these prisoners could no longer walk or stand. They were too weak. Death and disease hung in the air, lurking in and around every corner. There was no escaping it. The British called for more supplies right away.

The troops evacuated the camp, helping people move out of the mire. Soldiers dug large mass graves and made former SS guards fill them, carrying the dead on their backs. Former prisoners watched, some silently, others screaming at their Nazi tormentors. The British captured it on film. Those yelling are almost all women, full of so much loss and contempt. Only one male survivor is seen clearly in the footage. He is balled up on the ground, knees to chest, rocking back and forth in prayer, tears or both.

In another film from the camp, a British army chaplain stands in front of a mass grave and gives his testimony. "I've been here eight days, and never in my life have I seen such damnable ghastliness. This morning we buried over five thousand bodies, we don't know who they are. Behind me, you can see a pit, which will contain another five thousand. There are two others like it in preparation."[15] Thousands of lives, all cut short by starvation, the violence of neglect. The man's head stays low, his hands pushed deep in his pockets.

Those who did survive were given food, clothes, and medical treatment. Blimchu was wary of the food, packed in tins, and took only the chocolate and cigarettes from the soldiers, nothing else. She gave the chocolate to Golda and smoked the cigarettes herself, the start of a lifelong habit. Her skepticism over the food likely saved both of their lives. Much of the food the soldiers handed out—stew made from army rations, tinned beef, pork, bacon and sausage, plus hard biscuits—was too rich for starved, empty stomachs. Their health was too far-gone to process the food, their bodies too weak. Approximately 13,000 people died in the days after liberation, including more than 2,000 who tried the food.

To limit the continued spread of disease, the British cleared all the buildings on site. A "human laundry" was set up in a cavalry stable where German nurses were forced to wash, shave, and dust former camp prisoners with DDT.[16] The men and women were then wrapped in blankets and moved to makeshift hospital wards. With the buildings of Bergen Belsen cleared out, the British set the structures ablaze—long orange flames lashing the floors, walls and roofs. Former prisoners who were well enough to stand watched the camp burn from a distance. Their old barracks smoldered, smoked, and fell to dirt. Nazi flags were torched, everything razed. Fire consumed it all, burning, burning, until there was nothing left to burn. There was nothing left to wreck anymore.

FIFTEEN

— Somebody come running in, *This is the American, they gonna save us, they gonna save us*. It took awhile. He landed. Right away the American gave us candy and nylons, a little clothes, babushkas. They lined us up, get up, get up. They put us in another camp. More decent, liberated, you know? Over there they started giving us warm food and vitamins. You could shower, you could drink. Unbelievable. They made a kitchen, we eat regular food. They gave us vitamins.

We were sitting there for awhile. Long as you wanted you could stay there. Till you find any family, any friends, whatever. I ended up having typhus. Fever. Do you know what typhus is? Bad sickness. Sicker all the time. Scary stuff, I was there in my room laying there, sweating, screaming. *I'm thirsty, I'm thirsty, I'm thirsty.* They couldn't give me enough water. Laying in bed with a fever, nobody gave me a drink of water or anything. They were afraid to come next to me. What I went through. Ay ay ay.

There was an older man, talking to my cousin. Saw how I suffered, with a fever and everything. He made me drink water, he bring a bath cloth to put on my forehead, took me to the toilet, made sure I drink. He says, *It's going to go by in a few days, take it easy, it's gonna go by, don't worry*. In Jewish, he telling me, you know. He was a Polish guy from Poland. That's how it went on. He come and took me to the toilet, he gave me water to drink. He told me, *Lay down. You're gonna get over it, you're gonna be fine. Take the medicine, take the vitamins*. He looked after me like a father and child. I looked for him after the war to thank him. If not for that man, I would never have made it. Unbelievable.

Well, I got over that too and I ended up: earache, it was hurting me so bad. Over here, it was like a hammer. And what can I do? What can I do? There's no doctor coming to me. They told me, *Go there. There is a doctor with office. Go there and tell him to take a look. You can't take it anymore, the pain*. And I went by myself. I am surprised that I dared to go but I was so bad in pain, I had to go.

I went in the building, I opened the door, I said, *Ugh ugh, my head, my head*. He said, *Come here, sit down*. Wait a while. He gave me a needle. Here I was terrified of the Germans, gave me a needle not to feel so much. I was so in pain, fighting, scared, you know. Then he said, *Go in the waiting room, sit, lay down*. After I lay down, he put a box over my head. Light bulbs. They heat up my head, to see what anything left, bad thing in my head. Can you imagine how terrified I was? It wasn't too hot, it was lukewarm but I had to keep my head underneath till they come and got me. They examined me again and again to see if everything cleared up, I have no more. Some infection I must've had. It was so painful. Even now, I feel like a needle in my head, coming through. I have to be very careful with my ears. Nothing I can do. It's gone.

Memories, bad memories I have.

Somebody told me, *Your brother is home*. So what else I did? We hurry home to see him. Somebody said a lie. It's not true. We come home to Sighet, but nobody there. No place to stay, nothing to eat. Nothing to have a place to lay down. I heard my aunt is staying with an old man, it was some relative she was taking care of. And she said, *You come here, I take care of you.* So I stayed there. Till finally I was hearing nothing, nothing, couldn't find my brother. Anybody we ask, they couldn't find anybody.

There was two people who was driving a car, so they took me to go see the house. I said, *I have to go, I have to go.* So I went to see the house. Was no house. Nothing but dirt. Everything broken, taken apart. Nothing left. Of course I cried. I was all yellow. Scary. Pain, you know. Shock. We came back home. And I told my...unbelievable. Happened like that.

SIXTEEN

Golda and Blimchu returned to Romania after liberation and found their hometown in shambles. It had only been a year and yet everything had changed. Everything was different. The sisters were orphans and refugees, barely over their typhus. They had no home or belongings of any kind. No parents or grandparents. They were Jewish in a time and place where Jewish people were not welcome. They were women in a time and place where women had few ways to support themselves, the options severely limited. But also: they weren't women, not yet anyway, but teenage girls. Uneducated teenage girls. Malnourished teenage girls. Heartbroken teenage girls.

I've always wondered about this part of Bubbie's life, the gap between her leaving the camps and her leaving Europe. I couldn't imagine what she did, how she moved up and out of the strife. The suddenness of freedom, and the immediate limitations of it, must have been bewildering. She was only fourteen years old. When I was fourteen, I was building toothpick bridges for science class and learning how to tie a double-figure eight knot at the climbing gym. I couldn't fathom being so young and feeling so worn, stranded at the helm. Golda had no choice but to confront the world in front of her, find a way through the maddening storm.

Before returning to Romania, Golda and Blimchu had stayed in the displaced persons camp at the foot of

Bergen-Belsen with thousands of other refugees. They'd lived at the DP camp for several months, fighting the damage that disease, infection and a year's worth of starvation had left upon their ravaged bodies. It was an excruciating process, trying to heal, a process full of fitful nights and deprived, shaky days. They didn't know when they'd get better, or if they would at all. Everything was difficult: eating, drinking, sleeping, walking, going to the bathroom. But slowly, with time and the help of kind strangers, recovery became less of a challenge and more of a bore. They laid in bed. They slept. They drank water. They rolled over. As their bodies regained their natural strength and energy, the sisters began moving around more. Golda and Blimchu passed their later days at the DP camp meeting other young, homeless survivors like themselves, of which there were many. They sat on the floor with them, talking and playing games in a big circle. Spin the Bottle was one of the more popular choices amongst the group. After everything they went through, they were still teenagers. And resourceful ones at that. A couple people, an empty bottle and a little floor space and they were good to go.

One day, between resting and socializing, Golda was presented with an option for her future that had never crossed her mind before: international adoption. If she said yes to the offer, she'd be sent to Sweden where she'd be placed with a family or in a communal care home. It was a chance for a fresh start, a guarantee of food, safety and a little more childhood. However, the program came with one major drawback. Blimchu was eighteen and did not meet the program's age limitations, meaning if Golda decided to go, she would have to go alone.

Several years after my trip to Florida, I was able to glimpse these two options, what they meant and where they led. *All the Horrors of War,* a book by Bernice Lerner, combines the story of the British doctor who liberated Bergen-Belsen with that of one of the camp's survivors, a teenage girl originally from Sighet, Romania, the author's mother Ruth Mermelstein. I couldn't believe it. Ruth had been exactly where Bubbie had—Auschwitz, Christianstadt, Bergen-Belsen. She too survived with an older sister at her side, the rest of their immediate family killed. After the war, she went to Sweden and lived in a care home. I read the book the way one eats hard candy: all at once, savoring. I wrote Bernice an email and she told me Ruth was still alive. Before I knew it, we had arranged a phone call between the two women.

Though they didn't recall one another, Ruth and Golda were stunned to meet. My mom and I were with Bubbie in her apartment and put the phone on speaker. The women compared stories from every stage of their lives. Ruth had a vivid memory and spoke without hesitation, leading the conversation throughout the call. She asked Golda what street she grew up on in Sighet, then shared memories of walking down that street as a child. They passed names back and forth, names of other people in the camps with them, old friends and neighbors. They knew about half of the same people. Ruth told Golda that she moved to Sweden after the war. Bubbie nodded. "I almost went to Sweden, too. Almost."

"You should've. You should've come to Sweden," Ruth said. "You decided not to go to Sweden?" She was dumbfounded. Sweden had been a safe haven for her, a place to recuperate and recover.

"No, I went home to look for family," Bubbie said.

Ruth's voice was resolute. "I never wanted to go back. My children went back to Sighet, both my daughters went back to Sighet...and for me, it's death. For me, Sighet is death. Because nobody that I knew would be still alive."

"You're right," Bubbie said, "you're right."

Ruth spent ten years in Sweden after the war, recovering from her tuberculosis, working odd jobs and taking classes. Like Golda, she had been pulled out of school when she was young to help out at home. She used her time in Sweden to catch up, taking enough adult education courses to earn her high school diploma by the age of twenty-five. Through the aid of the Swedish Red Cross, Ruth grew into herself in Sweden, able to access medical care, work, and education. She even went to the opera on occasion. So, there it was: the other path, what could have been.

For Golda, there would be no Sweden. She could not bear the thought of being separated from her sister. How could she? Blimchu had been her lifeline, her ally, the one who stayed by her side when there was no one else, who told her when to leave the barracks at Christianstadt and hide. She was clever and caring, steadfast and strong. The sisters endured every threat together, every transport, every cold and hungry night in army-grade structures. They split their food with each other and shared beds of snow. They kept each other alive. Besides, what Golda craved most was not another unfamiliar place. She wanted her own home, her own family, the ones she knew and loved. The dream of reuniting with her older brothers was all-consuming. She had to try. In the end, it was not a difficult decision. After months in the DP camp,

Golda and Blimchu packed their bags and headed to the train station, leaving the camp as one.

At the train station, the sisters were overwhelmed by the rush and commotion. They found their train, but it was leaving. Golda and Blimchu sprinted for it, and Golda managed to throw her bag on board before they realized it was the wrong train. The train sped away and Golda was left without any luggage. The few items of clothing she had acquired were gone, but luckily she could still borrow from Blimchu. She still had her sister. The girls boarded the next train, the right one, relieved to be on their way. It was a 900-mile journey back home.

Upon arriving in Sighet, the sisters were greeted by a relative ghost town. There were no more busy shops and streets, no crowded marketplaces with people rushing about, making deals before sundown. Faces they did not recognize roamed the streets, eyes empty, searching as they searched. The population was bizarre and uneven: no one older than fifty, no one younger than Golda. Walking the streets of Sighet, the sisters realized they had no place to go. Of their large extended family, almost no one had survived the camps. However, they knew at least one relative who had. Aunt Suri, who had babysat them in what now seemed like another lifetime, had also made it out of the war alive. She too had been in the displaced persons camp at Bergen-Belsen, but had managed to leave before them, returning to Sighet when it was even emptier. There, incredibly, she reunited with an older relative and found a small one-bedroom apartment for them both to live in while she shepherded him back to good health. Suri suggested the girls stay with them in the apartment, too. She'd be able to offer them shelter there, but little else. Like them, she had nothing to her name. The girls didn't hesitate to say yes. They moved in right away, grateful for their aunt's kindness.

More people returned to the town, coming from concentration, forced labor, and displaced persons camps across Europe. Everyone was looking for someone—a parent, a husband, a sister, a girlfriend, a cousin, a brother, a friend. They couldn't have known it at the time, but of the 14,000 Jews deported from Sighet the previous spring, only several hundred had survived. Those who returned passed news back and forth over who was alive, who was dead, and who was still missing. Much more was unknown than known, but slowly information trickled into town. The surviving Jews started to piece together the scale of the devastation story by story, heartbreak by heartbreak. The girls shared the fates of the few they had seen in the camps and pressed other people for news on their brothers, Bumme and Mechel. They were given some small hopes, false starts and eventually, nothing at all. They already knew that their younger siblings, their mom, her dad, and their grandma Malka were gone. It was only with time that Golda and Blimchu would learn what happened to each of their brothers. The news would prove to be shattering.

The brothers, like their sisters, had endured many months of the same dangers and risks, the same deprivation. Only they'd done it alone. Due to their age difference, Bumme had been forced to join a Hungarian labor battalion, conscripted by the army earlier in the war, while Mechel had not. Mechel had been too young at the time. Instead, he was swept up in the Germans' raid on the town, sent to Auschwitz with the rest of his family and separated from them upon entering the camp. He was shipped to a Nazi labor camp months later, much like his sisters had been. Though the brothers were in the hands of different captors, both worked long, body-breaking days as forced laborers, receiving no proper gear, training, or sustenance. Mechel labored for a year, Bumme for two and a half. What type of work either brother did or where they did it is not known. No records remain. What is known is that like their sisters, both Bumme and Mechel made it to the end of the war. They both saw liberation, a single breath of freedom. But that was it. Unlike their sisters, they would go no further.

After his release from the Hungarian Labor Service, Bumme, the baker's apprentice, decided to make his way back to Sighet. While he was en route, a group of Hungarian fascists, part of the extremist Arrow Cross Party, caught him. He had been set free and yet still was being hunted. He was still wanted for existing in the larger world. The Arrow Cross men placed Bumme in a line of men along the Danube River in Budapest, Hungary. They ordered everyone to remove their shoes and set them along the river's banks. Moving from one end of the line to the other, they shot the men down one by one. Their bodies fell into the water like dominos, drifting away before the advancing Soviet troops could spot them. The men's leftover shoes, worn and dirty things, were collected afterwards by the Arrow Cross militiamen and traded on the black market for whatever they could get.

Mechel, the brother between Golda and Blimchu in age, did not die by bullet and water, but from starvation and disease. He too had ended up at Bergen-Belsen, likely via a similar death march as the one his sisters had endured. Despite being held in the same camp at the end of the war, the three never saw one another or knew how close they were. Mechel fell ill amidst the squalor of the camp, turning weaker and weaker from a lack of food. He was all but bones. When the camp was liberated and he was given food to eat, his stomach could not process it. He was desperately hungry, but no longer able to digest the most basic nutrients. He ended up dying, either from starvation itself, from illness, or from the last thing he tried to consume, a simple brown potato.

Golda struggled to eat after learning her brother's fate. Still, the girls had their aunt. Suri was a hard-working woman and did her best to care for her sister's daughters. She too felt the emptiness all around them. Suri washed the girls' hair at night and scavenged during the day to put food on the table. Eventually, she found help in the form of a husband. Shortly after the girls moved in with her, Suri married a leatherworker. Her new spouse joined them in the apartment, bringing along a new source of income as well as some unusually potent smells. His craft called for strong chemicals, salt brines and rancid tanning agents, not to mention the hides of dead animals. His leatherwork filled the tiny apartment with stench. It also attracted mice, which Golda found scurrying across her bed late at night and into the early morning.

Though Golda and Blimchu were much younger than their aunt, the pressure to get married reached them too. Many men, having lost their beloveds in the war, were eager to start anew. They hounded the sisters, stalking them outright. One man in particular had his eye on Golda. He was significantly older than her and would not let up. One day, while Golda was out in town, the man followed behind her to figure out where she was living. Later, when he knocked on the apartment door and asked to see her, Golda slipped out the window to escape. The sisters were still pale-faced teenagers, too young to be wives and mothers. They had gone from corpse-like to highly coveted in the blink of an eye.

Though neither one of them liked this sudden attention, Blimchu was especially leery. Before the war she had been social and friendly, eager to get out of the house and meet new people, but now she was always on edge. She kept her guard up in new situations and made sure to look out for her sister, becoming as protective of Golda as her older brother had once been of her. Later in life, she would struggle with her mental health in ways Golda never would, mumbling under her breath, talking to herself, afraid someone was out to get her. As the older sister, she had taken the brunt of the camps, and later she paid for it.

During their time in Sighet, the girls reunited with a cousin on their dad's side of the family, a woman named Helen Stein. Helen was older than both of them and already had a family of her own, living with her soon-to-be husband, his mother and his young son Marcel. They too resided in Romania, but in Timișoara, a city hundreds of miles south of Sighet. Though the fascist Iron Guard militia had operated in and around Timișoara, the Nazis never managed to reach it, so there had never been any deportations, no cattle cars to Poland. The Jews had suffered great prejudice there, but not mass persecution, meaning by the standards of the day, they had not suffered at all. Helen offered for the girls to stay with her and her new family for a while. To get away from the mice and the men, the girls said yes.

The three took a train to Helen's city, stopping in a hotel along the way, the first time Golda and Blimchu had ever stayed in one. Helen, who accompanied them, treated them to dinner. They ate fish that night, a lavish, otherworldly feast in their eyes. They savored every bite.

When the sun rose the following morning, the three continued on their way until they reached Timişoara. At first blush, the girls were taken aback by the big, beautiful homes, the lively action of the city Helen called home. To them, it was the most charming, exciting place they'd ever been.

The Steins operated a bakery in Timişoara and were doing well, thanks in large part to Helen's knack for business. While her fiancé baked bread in the kitchen, she developed a system for delivery by bike, reaching more customers by bringing their orders straight to their doorsteps—a service few bakeries in the area offered. The bike also came in handy for getting home and back. The family lived several miles away from the bakery in a complex with an open courtyard, ten apartment units, and a single bathroom for all to share. Helen's mother-in-law owned the building, which was always bustling with friends and family who either lived there, were staying for a while or were simply passing through. For dinner, the family turned one of the bedrooms into a temporary dining room in order to accommodate everyone present. Later, if there wasn't enough space for everyone to lay their heads down and sleep for the night, a small group was sent back to the bakery to rest in the warmth of the hearth.

Once the girls settled in Timişoara, Blimchu began to work at the family bakery. Golda stayed back, helping out around the Steins' home when she felt well and resting when she didn't. She was still in recovery from typhus. But even in Timişoara, nearly 250 miles south of their hometown, the girls got looks. Men came knocking on the door for them, and several went so far as to ask Helen for her permission to marry one of them. She said yes, but added that it was not her decision to make. The sisters were quick to speak for themselves. They said no.

After a full year of living with their cousin, Golda and Blimchu decided to move back to Sighet. It was time for them to return home. Blimchu moved in with a friend of hers who'd had a baby and needed extra help around the house. Golda moved in with another girl, single and closer to her in age. Though the sisters were no longer living together, they stayed close and trusted each other in ways they could trust no one else. They went out to social events together, some with live music and dancing, others with Zionist speakers, activists in support of establishing a Jewish state. Though Blimchu could be reserved and nervous, Golda was outgoing and sociable, happy to be around other people after being isolated for so long. She loved going out and meeting new people. Aunt Suri warned the girls to be careful when they attended these events in town. She told them to kiss no one. This was the only dating advice they'd ever receive.

After one of these nights out, a man asked Golda's roommate for her address. He had enjoyed dancing with Golda and now wanted to ask for her hand in marriage. But Golda's roommate did not know his intentions. She assumed he wanted their address so he could ask for her hand in marriage, not Golda's. The roommate was smitten, giddy at the thought of a proposal. Upon the man's arrival at their apartment, confusion fell over everyone, forcing him to clarify which girl he wanted to marry. Golda's roommate seethed at the feeling of betrayal. Right away, Golda turned the man down, which seemed to make matters worse between her and her roommate. Tensions mounted, growing worse over the coming days. Golda had no choice but to move again. She had no true home, no place to call her own. Even back in

Sighet, stability was still a distant fantasy. She went back to the only place she could think of—Aunt Suri's foul-smelling, mouse-infested apartment.

For Golda, it was clear she couldn't evade marriage forever. Matrimony was her only path forward, her only path anywhere. She was impoverished and illiterate, without any power or means to pave her own way. She kept attending social events and speeches in town until one night she met a man there who ran his own grocery store. He was older than her, but not by as much as some of the other men had been. He was a handsome guy, slender too. Originally from Sighet, the man was one of five siblings, four brothers who survived the war and one sister who had died before it'd begun. Though he had lived, many of his close friends and relatives had not, including his long-time girlfriend. After some waiting and hoping, fiendish questioning and desperate, desperate praying, he was now trying to move on from their deaths. He wanted to find a way to enjoy the life that lay before him. It would not be an easy task. He'd lost his parents, his love, good friends, and several toes. The man's name was Benti Indig.

Benti had not been in the concentration camps, but when Bubbie told me he was in the "soldier's war," I didn't know what that meant either. After months of research, I put it together. Like Golda's brother Bumme, Benti had been drafted into one of the Hungarian army's forced labor units for the sole reason that he was Jewish. He was on the Eastern Front, made to do grueling work in service of the army—a laborer, not a soldier, but I suspect it was easier for everyone to think of it the other way around. Out of the 100,000 Hungarian Jewish men conscripted into forced labor, approximately 40,000 died in the war, largely on the Ukrainian steppes.[17]

◆

Like Golda's other suitors, Benti was drawn to her. He found her intelligent and pretty, a solid chance for a fresh start. Unlike her other suitors, he gave her a necklace and promised he'd always take her dancing. From there, the two started spending more time together. When Benti proposed that they get married, Golda hesitated but ultimately said yes. It was a sensible arrangement, a smart move, if not quite an act of love. They hadn't known each other very long. For the wedding, Golda found a white dress to borrow while Benti took care of the rest of the preparations. A small gathering of friends joined them, huddling together in Benti's backyard. She was seventeen years old the day they got married; he was twenty-five. Neither had parents.

Shortly after the wedding, both Golda and Blimchu decided to leave Sighet. Nothing was left for them in their wreck of a town. No future, no hope. It was their mom, after all, who had made Sighet their home, and she was no longer around. Instead Soviet soldiers walked the streets of the city, confirming the girls' sense of unease. Nearly all of the surviving Jews of Sighet were in a similar position. They had learned what they could from being back home and had nothing more to gain. It was not their home anymore. Many of these people, including Golda and Blimchu, found their way back to displaced persons camps. International organizations and Jewish agencies had been set up at these DP camps to provide refugees with food, clothing, a safe place to sleep and in some cases, vocational training. More importantly, these organizations aided with the emigration process, helping survivors find a more stable, permanent way of life. Through DP camps across Europe, most of the remaining Jews of Sighet moved to foreign, far-off places, individually and in droves, that year and all the years that followed, so that by 2002, only twenty Jews still called the town home.

Blimchu left first. Intrigued by the Zionist speakers she heard in town, she dreamed of moving to the emerging state of Israel. It became her singular goal, a symbol to mark the end of her suffering. Once her mind was set, it was set—a trait she likely picked up from Henia. Though Golda wanted to join, she couldn't. Her new husband had other plans. For Benti, the end goal had always been North America. His brothers were headed there, and he wanted nothing more than to join them. Golda could not convince him otherwise, nor could she convince Blimchu to go west with them. She didn't want to separate from her sister, but neither one could give up her plans. After surviving the war at one another's side, the sisters now had to do what they had never done before. They had to survive apart. Their farewell—how long it took, how many tears, promises, whispers, kisses—was not a story I was given.

To get to Israel, Blimchu first moved to a displaced persons camp in Ebelsberg, Austria. While waiting to be accepted for resettlement, she met a man at the camp and began dating him. His parents disapproved of their relationship because of her status as an orphan. She was humiliated by their scorn. How could people be so cruel? But the war had not softened anyone, not eased anyone's heart. Regardless of his parents, the two decided to marry. In 1949, they moved to Israel as husband and wife, joining Kibbutz Shefayim, a community settlement near the Mediterranean Sea, a few years later. Blimchu worked as a cook there. She had three children in total: Henia, Peritz and Tova. She would see her younger sister again, but not for many years.

After Blimchu left Romania, Golda and Benti packed up their meager belongings and left too. Benti sold his grocery store to fund the move. Golda bid her few remaining friends and relatives goodbye, but most had already left or were about to leave themselves. Aunt Suri and her husband moved to Israel; Helen and her family went to Israel, then the US, settling in Brooklyn. With her new groom at her side, Golda moved to Kirchseeon, Germany, a small village outside the DP camp in Munich. Of Benti's three brothers—Isaac, Jack, and Barry—two were already in Germany when the newlyweds arrived. Benti and Golda moved in with them, everyone squeezing into a small one-bedroom apartment.

Benti found a job as a driver inside the DP camp. His brothers both worked there as well. Meanwhile, Golda stayed in the apartment and prepared everyone's meals. Benti's family had become her family and she had become responsible for all the cooking and cleaning. This was new to her. Often, she was short on a few key ingredients and had to run to the market alone while the brothers were out at work for the day. To get around town, she relied on an old bicycle. Golda got to know the unfamiliar German roads, the bumps and bends, committing the market's location to memory.

Once, while riding her bicycle back to the apartment, Golda noticed everything felt a little shaky. She jumped off and examined the bike. Something was wrong and right away, she saw what it was. Someone had loosened all the screws on her bike while she had been buying produce in the market. She was a Jew in post-war Germany and lest she forget, the *post-* part was still new.

Despite their neighbors' hostilities, Benti and Golda carried on. They worked and cooked and applied for resettlement. Benti filled out the paperwork. He wanted to go to the United States, but the two would accept whatever country offered to take them in. Anything to leave Europe, the home of their loss and misery. Both of Benti's brothers received word they'd been accepted for emigration to Canada. They left Golda and Benti behind in Germany with nothing to do but wait and see if they too would have such luck.

While living outside Munich, Golda became pregnant with her first child. She was eighteen years old. At nine months, she began to feel contractions, slow ones, steady ones, and knew it was time. The baby was on its way. She and Benti hurried to the closest hospital, catching a train to get there. When they arrived, the nurses wouldn't let them in. They said it was too early. The couple, unable to afford another train ride home and back, found seats in the waiting room. They sat there and waited, unsure when—or if—they'd be admitted.

Finally Golda was granted a room. The nurses walked her down a long hallway to a clean, white space. Lying flat on a narrow hospital bed, she pushed. Perspiration pooled on her forehead and in her thick, brown hair. She was in labor for many hours. The pain of it felt unbearable to her. Sharp, mean. No matter. This was it. She pushed and pushed and pushed, and there she was, a baby girl. The nurse wrapped the baby in her arms and took her to her station to clean her up.

Still sweating, in anguish, Golda called out. "Mom," she cried. "My mom, my mom! I want my mom!"

The nurse held out the baby, bundled in thin white linens, and placed her in Golda's arms. "You're the mom now."

SEVENTEEN

— And what became of me? I heard they making a speech about coming to Israel, they want everybody to come to Israel. They making speeches, we should all come to Israel. So we all went, we listen to what they had to say. And on the way home, Benti walked me home. I was scared. Everyone was saying, oh he's a good guy, he's a nice guy. So he walked me home. He says, *Is there anybody you can ask what you can do if someone asks you to marry him? Got someone to talk to about that?*

I said, I can talk for myself. You know.

There was so many people who wanted to marry me, there wasn't too many girls coming home. Older men, all kinds of men asking to get married. So what can I do? I didn't say I want to marry you or anything. Forty-eight hours, it'd be great if he brings me a necklace. I was sitting by my aunt in the place and her husband was making leather, it was such a smell to make the leather. Shoes and whatever. I was staying there for a while. He come to visit. My aunt said, *He looks like a nice guy. He has a home, he has a store. And he comes from a good family*. That's it.

— Had he been in the war too?

— He was. Soldier's war. He ended up having frozen feet, the toes from the feet pulled down themselves.

— He was a soldier?

— In the end. You know, they put the soldiers to cut trees. To clean up the…

— So, he wasn't a prisoner?

— Not in concentration camp. It was like a group, like an army.

— He was in the army.

— And he had one friend. They were carrying long trees, here and there, from one place to another. And his friend stayed on the other end on the tree that they carry. He dropped down the tree, the tree went on his friend. And he was so miserable. He took it very hard. He came home all swollen from the camp. And the friends tried to help: get a place to stay, little business. But that's how he feel. What you gonna do?

— How old were you when you…

— Thirteen year old!

— So fourteen when the liberation…

— Small, skinny.

— How old were you when you got married?

— Seventeen.

— So, you had three years between.

— Unbelievable. Unbelievable. After a few months, we are married. I was safe but not happy. I was safe. I had a place to stay. I learned a little from the neighbors, did what I could to survive.

He had brothers in Germany. They said, *Come to Germany, we're gonna go to America, you'll have a better life.* So what now? What my husband did? He sold everything and we went. We went. He had two brothers there and I was the one staying home cooking and my husband find a job with the Americans. He was delivering soap and what needed to the people of the camp. He had a little bit of money. He brought something home—soap, whatever he could, he come home with. That was the end of the concentration camp, struggling from one end to the other.

From there we applied to Canada, United States. Whatever came soon, we accepted that. We had Canada right away because I was Czechoslovakia-born, I'm in quota. And I tell you, what a miserable life. In Germany to come to Canada. Wasn't easy.

EIGHTEEN

Hours after I lost Bubbie at the hair salon that first full day in Florida, there was an afternoon card game. Bubbie loved playing cards, gin rummy being her favorite game. She uncapped a tube of red lipstick and told me a friend of hers was going to join us to play. This, I realized later, was the reason she'd changed her mind about getting her hair done. Gotta look good for company.

When her friend arrived, the three of us sat down at the dining room table and Bubbie cracked open a deck of cards. I'd been playing gin rummy with her since I was a kid and knew the game well, but every time we played together, the rules seemed to change on me. She couldn't help it. She was always adding nuances, picking up new variations, altering the game as I knew it. We had played with ten cards and fourteen, with pocket change, with tiles, with open hands and closed. This time, we played with points and money. Bubbie explained to me that you needed fifty points before you could lay your cards down, which would save you a nickel if you didn't win later. She filled me in on the rules as we played, and not before. I stayed a step behind the other two, trying to catch up and learn the rules to this game I thought I knew.

After a few muddled hands, the phone rang, a loud trill coursing through the condo. It was one of Bubbie's neighbors calling, a chatty gray-haired woman named Elizabeth. We paused our playing and Bubbie answered the call, listening to Elizabeth talk, nodding and uh-huhing along. The two were nothing alike—one was tall and hailed from Spain, the other short, round and Romanian—but they were close in age and far from family, and because of this, they had become good friends. They looked out for one another, sharing ingredients, saving leftovers, and passing news back and forth. Elizabeth was especially good at getting dirt on the building, her ear always to the ground. If she wasn't a detective or investigative reporter in an earlier life, then she should have been.

While listening to Elizabeth, Bubbie turned toward me. Apparently, there was an emergency happening on the fourth floor. "A man cut himself and needs help," she said, her ear pressed to the phone. "You'll go?"

"Oh," I replied with my usual eloquence. "Sure."

I set my cards down and hurried to the elevator, letting the other two finish the game without me. I rode the elevator down to Elizabeth's condo, a similar sized unit on the seventh floor. She wanted to accompany me since I had never met the bleeding man before, a logic I fully agreed with. I was just learning the details of the incident: the man's name was Julian, today happened to be his eighty-ninth birthday, and the severity of his injury was still unknown.

When I knocked on Elizabeth's door, she invited me in. When she said, "Thank you so much for helping, I can't stand the sight of blood," I said of course, leaving out the small detail that I too was not a huge fan. When she gave me a tour of her place, complete with origin stories for each and every plant on the balcony, I said, "Should we go check on Julian?" She agreed and grabbed her purse.

I had no idea what Bubbie had signed me up for. In the rush of everything, I'd forgotten how prone to reaction she could be, how willing she was to move at a moment's notice. She had a knack for turning nothing into something, but I never knew when it was a something and when it was a nothing.

The fourth floor looked like the seventh floor, which looked like the fifteenth. They were all windowless and plain with pale yellow walls and emergency staircases at either end. We walked to Julian's apartment halfway down the hall and I knocked on the door. There was no answer. We waited for half a minute, then I knocked a little louder, a little more forcefully. I could feel the thump of my heartbeat grow faster.

Still, there was no answer. I had my phone on me and gave it to Elizabeth to call Julian's landline. Luckily, she knew his number by heart. She was well connected in the building, a mother hen at her roost. The phone rang inside the apartment loudly enough that we could both hear it from the hall. It kept ringing and ringing, but no one picked up. I grew more concerned by the second.

"You know, he's hard of hearing," Elizabeth said, heading back to the elevators. "That's probably it."

"Yeah, maybe." I did not feel so sure. Hadn't Bubbie said it was an emergency? That he needed help? Something about this did not feel right. Elizabeth and I agreed to try again in thirty minutes. If we couldn't get ahold of Julian then, I quietly planned to call 911 and get real help.

I returned to Bubbie's condo. Her friend had left by then, so it was just the two of us. As she straightened up the dining room and put away the cards, I gave her the scoop on Julian. The knock, the call, the silence. Like Elizabeth, she seemed unfazed.

A half hour later, I took the elevator back to Elizabeth's unit. Instead of going down to the fourth floor again, she called Julian from her kitchen phone. I tapped my fingers against my leg as it rang. This time, he picked up. It turned out he had heard our call before, but had chosen not to answer it because he'd been in the tub and didn't want to slip on the tile, hurting himself worse. Apparently he had a small cut on his leg and he already managed to bandage it himself. In fact, he said we shouldn't come by anymore because he was still naked, thank you very much.

I left Elizabeth's apartment, exhausted from so much needless action and worry. It was a cut. A paper cut on an old man's leg. It was nothing at all. I pressed the up button at the elevator bank and returned to Bubbie's floor.

I couldn't help but feel frustrated. Why had Bubbie sent me? Why had she told me it was an emergency? Couldn't she have taken a beat and asked for more information? I wanted to understand how she thought, the moves she made. They felt inexplicable to me, unnecessary and impulsive. She had confounded me throughout my trip, doing the exact opposite of what I would have done in nearly every situation. It kept happening, again and again, and I could not figure out why.

I recalled our first interview, the way her eyes had narrowed and her voice boomed. How startled I had been to see such anger and hurt in her. She never let her anger and hurt show, not to me. Our normal routine had always been care packages and phone calls, hot food and big hugs. She sent me so many packages when I was in college that I bought blank nametags so I could pre-write my address for her and send her a pack at a time. Learning of her wartime experiences gave me a new frame in which to see her. The past was context, or could be, if I was willing to hold it.

When Bubbie was ten years old, her town changed countries. Five years later it changed back. Her youth had been filled with events beyond her control, political ones, personal ones, havoc forever on the horizon. She could only watch as things shifted and shattered around her. Nothing ever made sense. Her dad, the strong one, became a memory. Her mom, the one who stayed home, became a visitor, traveling to make ends meet. Her brother Bumme, the baker, became a forced laborer for the state. Her neighborhood became a ghetto. Her synagogue became a holding pen. Her hair became a German soldier's socks. Her stomach became empty. Her house became rubble. Her family became smoke. The chaos was unceasing.

And she became accustomed to that chaos. It shaped her, the volatility and violence, the frequency, forging her into the woman she was now. It forged others, too. In a study conducted in the Czech Republic, neurologists examined the brain function of a group of Holocaust survivors using MRI technology. They wanted to know if surviving the Holocaust had a life-long psychological and biological effect. What they found was that, compared with controls, survivors showed "a significant decreased volume of grey matter in the brain."[18] Having less grey matter affected their memory, motivation, emotion, stress response, learning and behavior. In other words, everything. The Czech study also found that younger survivors were likely to have less grey matter than older ones, suggesting that the human brain is more vulnerable to stress during its development. For child survivors like Bubbie, the trauma was foundational.

In all my writing and research, my desperation to understand her choices and the reasons she made them, I discovered another study that seemed to have met her and sat at her table. The research study, conducted in Israel, considered attachment and traumatic stress among female Holocaust survivors specifically. It found that female survivors had high levels of avoidant behavior, intrusive thoughts, unusual beliefs, autonomic anxiety, cognitive worry, and an unresolved state of mind.[19] Of course her mind was unresolved. She never knew what was around the next corner. She never knew what would bend and what would break.

As Hédi Fried, a fellow survivor from Sighet, writes in her book *Questions I Am Asked About the Holocaust*, "There was no logic in the camp; you never knew where to be, or not to be, in order to survive."[20] Holocaust survivors, no matter their background, had to adapt to the absence of logic, the sheer pandemonium of persecution and war. Everything was unstable: food, work, safety, sleep. The only thing one could get used to was not being used to anything at all.

How does a person handle so much uncertainty? How does one cope with a conveyor belt of chaos? As a young woman, Bubbie had no guides, no role models to follow or resources to consult. "What can you do?" she often said, more as a form of acceptance or resignation than as an actual question. She had learned to respond to stress as she would any other unexpected guest. She unfurled the welcome mat and invited it in.

My whole life, I watched as Bubbie embraced chaos. I saw it in how she reacted on a dime, the way she solved problems by making more. I saw it in the way she jumped around in action and thought, following tangents rather than plans. There were never plans. Her illiteracy compounded her impulsivity, ensuring she had less information than those around her. I saw it in how she fretted, misheard, speculated and blamed. I saw it in how she communicated, or miscommunicated, or didn't bother to communicate in the first place. She was always scattered like this, unable to focus. Chaos was an intruder so frequent in her life, she didn't know how to operate without it. It became a reliable motivator for her, a close companion, a force as familiar as anything else.

I did not feel the same. Chaos did not propel me forward; it stressed me out. I had no appreciation for running around, worrying myself from the fifteenth floor to the seventh to the fourth. My preference was always for planning ahead, thinking things through, being careful and cautious. But the more I thought about the incident, the more I doubted myself. Had Bubbie used the word "emergency," or had I added that in my head? Had I translated her impulse to help, swift but impassive, into my own high-octane anxiety? She may have been disengaged, but I was live-wired. Her detachment kindled a kind of sensitivity in me, aware and attentive, desperate to do right. I was used to having some semblance of control in my life, but here, in humid south Florida, I felt like I had none. My head throbbed. It was the smallest taste of the stress Bubbie knew, how she coped, the call and response. I opened the door to her place, slipped off my sandals and made a beeline for the couch. She sat next to me.

"Busy day," she said, putting her feet up. I couldn't disagree.

NINETEEN

When I asked Bubbie about living in Canada, she struggled to give me an answer. She had never given it much thought before. Canada was Canada. I could relate. My family made occasional trips to Ontario to visit relatives when I was young and my main memories were of the Coffee Crisp candy bars I ate there. Still, I wanted to know more about this chapter of Bubbie's life, the transition from refugee to raising a family. So few stories of survival speak of the after, when the immediate danger has ended and the longer, harder work must begin. In her memoir *The Man Who Could Move Clouds*, Ingrid Rojas Contreras recalls the violence she faced growing up in Colombia and says, "There is surviving, and then there is surviving the surviving. There is a version of the story in which a survivor doesn't make it; and a version in which a survivor is remade."[21] None of Bubbie's story was guaranteed. To make it in North America, she had to allow herself to be remade, to lose as much as she might gain. She had to seek change, constant, perpetual change, and confront the uncertainty of every new thing, every unfamiliar object and person and custom and food. She had to face a world unlike the one she knew to live in a world unlike the one she knew.

My grandparents arrived in Canada in the spring of 1950. After living outside the DP camp in Munich for several years, Benti and Golda were granted approval to leave the country. Weeks later, they boarded a decommissioned army ship and sailed across the Atlantic Ocean with their one-year-old daughter Hedi in their arms. The MSTS General McRae, as the ship was called, had been used years earlier for shuttling US troops around ports in Hawaii and the South Pacific. Now it operated in aid of the mass resettlement of refugees from that very same war. Benti, Golda and Hedi left Germany's shore with a hundred or so others, most of who were not Jewish. One month later, they arrived in Halifax, Nova Scotia. They stepped off the boat with no funds, prospects, or sense of what lay ahead—at this point, a familiar feeling.

The family of three moved to Windsor, Ontario to live with Benti's brother Barry and his wife Faigu until they could afford a place of their own. During the day, Benti searched for work while Golda stayed home and cared for their baby girl. In the evening, they took night classes to learn English—they did not yet know the language. Within a few years, their family grew: first a son, Harry; then a second daughter, Gail (my mom). They practiced their English with their kids, learning it alongside them. Eventually, they only spoke English to them. They wanted their children to know the language better than they did, to face less discrimination. And they succeeded: neither my mom, aunt, or uncle can speak any language besides English. They didn't know the languages their parents lived in, the ones their mom and dad spoke as children. Yiddish was an old world they were not allowed into. I have a collection of Yiddish words that I know—keppy, punim, shayna, kvetch—and that's it, a collection. I know no Hungarian or Romanian.

And yet, for my grandparents, these languages were home, especially Hungarian and Yiddish. They wove them into their other conversations, including with each other and with friends. The singsong rhythms filled their every day, going safely over the heads of their little ones. Golda and Benti's English improved over time, but still, an accent stuck to their sentences, casting a long Eastern European shadow over everything they said and did. They felt prejudice all around them. As their kids got older, they started turning to them for help. They dreaded paperwork and had their children fill out lengthy forms for them instead. There was so much, they found, that was easier when delegated. Once, a parent-teacher conference came up at school for their youngest daughter and they sent their eldest daughter in their place. She could handle it fine, they thought—probably in Yiddish.

I too have served as a messenger for my grandma. I've spoken for her, unscrambled, read, repeated, explained, expounded. I interpret what she's trying to get at and clarify it for others who might not know. Or, I render their words back to her in a simpler (read: louder) form. It's the work of translation and despite only speaking one language fluently, I know it well. Mediating, describing, relaying, connecting. It's what I'm doing right now.

Benti found a job at a window factory and the family moved into a small brick house on Goyeau Street. The three kids shared a bedroom; the two girls shared a bed. Money was tight and the family saved however they could. They rented rooms out to lodgers and Golda watched the neighbors' kids in addition to her own. Benti's three brothers all lived nearby. Together, with a handful of friends, they formed a mini enclave of Jewish refugees and survivors, Yiddish and Hungarian speakers who preferred paprika over poutine. As the youngest of the group, Golda was always learning from the others, trying to keep up. Her sisters-in-law taught her the basics of domestic life including sewing, crocheting, and cooking. They showed her the recipes they knew best, rich Hungarian ones with lots of salt. In no time, Golda could cook up a feast of her own. The families gathered regularly for dinner together, rotating between their homes and kitchens. They stayed close and stuck to what they knew, having no elders in their lives to turn to for guidance. They had each other and though that wasn't nearly enough, they made do.

After a few years in Canada, Benti secured a loan to open a restaurant. Ben's Coffee Shop, located on Wyandotte Street in downtown Windsor, was a modest diner with small tables and a line of squeaky round stools along the bar. The restaurant served the usual fare: hot coffee, grilled cheese, roast beef with gravy. Golda cooked cabbage rolls in the back—a mix of ground beef, rice, onion, and spices wrapped in cabbage and baked at a low temperature. Sometimes, she'd cook at home and bring the food down to the restaurant by bicycle. Other times, she'd bring my mom—a precocious little girl with a talent for ringing up customers at the register and selling them on extras like chocolate and cigarettes—along to the diner.

Golda became increasingly resourceful as a matter of necessity, a form of survival. For under a dollar, she made skirts and dresses for her daughters. She tailored the pieces with a beam of pride. Her daughters, however, did not always feel the same. In their eyes, Golda's ingenuity was more embarrassing than it was impressive, a marker of being poor and different. Once, as homework, Hedi's elementary school teacher asked the class to make a cloud from cotton balls and Golda pulled apart a Kotex pad instead. Hedi was mortified as her classmates called out what it was the next day at school, but it was the best her mom could give her.

The two generations were light-years apart. What seemed normal for one was outrageous to the other. Both Benti and Golda baffled their children. Were they inflexible? Or had they flexed so much, carried so much uncertainty, dealt with so much upheaval, that their muscles retracted, cold to more change? Benti, desperate to maintain family tradition, kept live chickens in the basement. When it was time for dinner, he took them to a kosher butcher shop in town to have them properly killed and cleaned. In went the clucking fowl and out came bare, featherless birds for Golda to season and bake. Once, he even kept a live fish in the family's bathtub before taking it to the butcher for a proper kosher killing. Nothing about this struck him as odd. Needless to say, the children did not invite friends to the house.

After more than a decade in Canada, my grandparents decided to emigrate once again. This move was short: from Windsor to Detroit, a bridge away. Still it was daunting. They had to sell Ben's Coffee Shop and their car in order to afford it. It was 1962 and once again, everything was new to them. They were starting over in an unfamiliar land, destined forever to be foreigners.

Benti worked to secure funds for a new restaurant in the States. He wanted to reopen his diner, or a version of it, in Detroit. While he planned his future restaurant venture, Golda took a job at General Motors to cover the family's expenses. On an assembly line at the GM Hamtramck plant, she learned to sew leather seats for Cadillac cars. It was intense, fast-paced factory work, but she was quick to find a rhythm to it. While working at

GM, she interacted with more people than she ever had before. The auto plant employed thousands of people from all walks of life. Golda came home after work having unintentionally picked up their accents—Italian ones, Southern ones—her own English improving in the process. Though she only took the job for the short term, she ended up staying with the company for thirty-one years. She moved up the ranks, at least those open to her, going from sewing on the factory line to cleaning executive offices.

The kids also adapted. They made new friends in school and learned to spell color without the u, the bulk of their language barrier. Harry picked up a newspaper route around the neighborhood (no longer the neighbourhood) and Hedi got her driver's permit through the local high school. She earned her Michigan driver's license shortly after that. Meanwhile, my mom attended primary school. It was there at Key Elementary that she was assigned to the same third-grade class as my dad. (Years later, they'd see each other at a party and he'd say, "I think we were in the same third-grade class.") My mom sunk herself into her schoolwork, reading everything she could get her hands on. Books were an escape for her, a way to block the noise of everything else.

Benti's diner flopped. The only spot in the city he could afford was crime-ridden, repelling more people than it attracted. He looked for other work, finding and losing a string of low-paying jobs. Nothing stuck. At the same time, Golda was rising, both socially and at work. No matter where she went, she was well-liked, connecting easily with others. Benti struggled to do the same. Where Golda was kind and helpful, he was mistrusting and cold. Where she was funny, he was serious. His normal speaking voice was a harsh booming shout, although more often than not he was silent and withdrawn. In the end, he decided to buy himself a taxicab. His car was black with white doors, red letters spelling the name of the taxi company on its sides. His number, 517, was mounted on top. As a taxi driver, he could work whenever and wherever he wanted and more importantly, without any colleagues or bosses.

The pain of the past surrounded Benti and Golda, a cloud they never understood but always felt. They hoped to move past their wartime experiences in the United States, a place they perceived as having endless opportunities. The thought of attaining something more allured them. But post-traumatic stress does not care where you hang your hat. The darkness of the past clung to them, even here, even now, leaving each to handle the ache and sorrow in their own way.

For Benti, tragedy was a lead weight. He sank into a deep depression and became sullen, weighed down by memories of the war and Hungarian Labor Service. They haunted him. He brooded over the past, over the people he had lost. His mental health worsened. When he felt like he couldn't get enough air in the house, he drilled holes in the kitchen cabinets. In he breathed heartache, out he breathed fury.

Golda was the opposite. She didn't stew, but surged. Though many of her friends stayed at home during the day to tend to their kids and kitchens, Golda kept working in the auto factory. She hitched rides to the plant with co-workers, sold jewelry under the table, took the kids to piano lessons, crocheted chunky afghans, patched old clothes, and made batch after batch of potato latkes for dinner. Being busy suited her. It was how she dealt, or rather how she didn't deal, with her losses. Trauma as fuel. Trauma as energy. Her feet were always moving.

The disparity in how the two handled their distress—his tendency to withdraw, her tendency to take charge—led to great friction between them. They fought over everything, in loud foreign words their kids could only guess at. There was no more dancing in the city center or friendly walks home. In their place grew resentment, jealousy and anger, emotions as regular as a morning cup of coffee. Their conversations could be vicious and accusatory. They separated several times, living together and apart, on and off. Golda weighed the idea of divorce, but never went through with it. Instead, the two stayed together and stayed fighting, a relationship made of hard words and ill tempers. They spared each other no grace.

And this is just what I've been told, what I'm allowed to know.

In every attempt at remembrance, there's forgetting. "Yes," Viet Thanh Nguyen writes, "remembering and forgetting entwine together, a double helix making us who we are, one never without the other."[22] We are built off our memories, what they hold and what they leak. How does one tell a leaky story? Well, there are no other kinds.

I wish I had more insight into this era of my grandma's life. I wish I knew more about her relationships and connections, what she shared with others and what she kept to herself. Did the Holocaust come up in conversation at work? Over dinner? In bed? I wish I had more nuance and interiority and detail and dialogue. I long for fiction, but am left with the blanks of real life. No one was willing to give me more than I could handle, or more than they could. My mom has so few memories from childhood, the details long since buried.

For Bubbie, it was all a blur. Everyone protected each other in this way: lose the things that hurt, then hurt over their loss.

For the most part, I wasn't there. I was not a witness, only a witness to a witness. Only a granddaughter. In Florida, I sought answers, but collected questions. There was so much I did not understand, so much I still don't understand. War is senseless after all, trauma confounding. Still, I scoured for ways to piece it together. I wanted to link then and now, to locate threads of connection from the floor of my grandma's condo and spool them into language, rich and clear. I was trying to shape a narrative, but in Bubbie's company, I shaped nothing. Memories came and went, stories flitted by, distractions found, errands run. I sighed a lot in Florida.

A part of me wondered if I might find something to help me tell Bubbie's story, some personal materials or handwritten notes. Maybe I'd stumble on a secret stack of letters tied up with string, or a faded black trunk stuffed with old files. I'd certainly read enough books like that—a dusty corner, an unassuming box, something dark inside. I couldn't help but imagine a diary. The image was alluring: a shelter for secrets, a place for feeling when life called for action. I imagined myself climbing a set of old attic stairs, wooden and worn, where a box filled with papers waited for me at the top. I wanted to clear the haze with prose. But I knew. There were no papers or boxes or old attic stairs. This was a condo building, and Bubbie didn't write.

But there was something else.

Back in Philadelphia I remembered an old video my parents kept in a bookcase in our basement, a VHS in a cardboard sleeve. I had watched it once, but had little memory of it. In 1997, somewhere in Miami Beach, the Shoah Foundation conducted an interview with Bubbie as part of a growing movement to preserve testimony of the Holocaust and other genocides. Our conversations were not her first time telling her story, and I thought I might learn something from this earlier attempt. How did a professional interviewer handle this history? How did a person with training make sense of the complexities of war and genocide? There may not have been any letters or diaries for me to find, but there was this, an outdated tape on a crowded shelf, packed in my parents' basement.

Founded by Steven Spielberg in 1994, the Shoah Foundation has interviewed witnesses and survivors of genocide in more than forty languages and sixty countries. The archives are a part of the University of Southern California and hold more than 55,000 audio-visual testimonies, testimonies chronicling life before, during, and after firsthand exposure to genocide. My dad dug up our copy of Bubbie's Shoah Foundation interview and converted it to a digital format for me. (Neither of us owned VHS players anymore.) Once he sent me the link, I downloaded the video onto my laptop. Bubbie appeared before me, her hair a dark brown again, heavy with hairspray. Her forehead, shiny and taut. Small good hoops hung from her ears. She looked great.

The interviewer, a woman with short blonde hair and good posture, appears at the start of the video. She talks in a slow monotone voice, delivering her questions as if part of an oral exam. Bubbie responds to her mechanical questioning with noticeable hesitation and a cold, mistrusting eye. She speaks in mumbles, her answers quiet and hard to make out. She is being cautious, guarded even, in a way I don't recognize, a way she never is on the phone with friends or at home with family.

As soon as the interviewer asks questions about violence, Bubbie jumps ahead, having so much to say and no good way to say it all. This interview, Bubbie told me later, was the first time she ever spoke in depth about what happened to her during the war, on tape or not. She didn't know how to pace herself, how to say everything she wanted to say. She didn't know what to say in the first place. When the Shoah Foundation interviewer asks her about instances of antisemitism from before the war, Bubbie rambles about rumors running through the town. The interviewer tries again, restating the question. "Do you recall any instances...happening before the war to you or your family?" Bubbie is quick to reply. "Before the war, the Nazis came to the house." This is not an instance from before the war; this is the war itself. This is May 1944. She doesn't care about delineations of time, of official dates and facts. She rushes through her memories, skipping over major details, offering only what she thinks the interviewer is interested in hearing. She is a complex, layered person, but she isn't sure if she can be. If she is allowed. At times, Bubbie smooths the truth out so much it is no longer true. When asked where she was born, she says Sighet, the town where she grew up, a town in a different country.

When it comes to her wartime experiences, including where she was and what she saw, details big and small get lost in a swell of old memories. She mixes up her words, saying bunkers, but meaning bunk beds. To describe the manual labor at Christianstadt, a camp she doesn't name, she speaks in a circular manner. "Some people used to go cut trees, lift for the train, to make room to make a train, cut wood, carry it, cleaning out the field, to make a train line." She has not processed these memories before, let alone shared them in English. At the time of the war, she didn't know a single word of English.

Bubbie becomes distraught the more she remembers, her eyes welling with the tears she has held in for half a century. At times, she is hard to hear, in part because of the audio quality and in part because she's murmuring through her sobs. Other times, she opens her mouth and nothing comes out. The interviewer appears to be lost in all of Bubbie's emotion, unable to navigate the larger story. She doesn't know what's there and what's not.

Once the interview falls off track, it only gets worse. A doorbell rings in the background, interrupting the taping. Moments later, the two restart, but the camera runs out of film and they have to stop again. Bubbie and the interviewer never find a rhythm to their conversation, a groove in which things might make some sense. Their only pathway is a choppy one, rambling and confusing, the kind you can't help but trip up on.

The tape ends with a showcase of photographs from throughout Bubbie's life. For some reason, she is hardly in them. In fact, I am in more of the photos than she is. One of the pictures is of me in a tree, a bright grin across my seven-year-old face. Why am I in a tree? What does that have to do with the war? With the three Nazi concentration camps she was held in, her year of starvation? I was surprised to see myself in the film, fingers wrapped around bark, hair as wild as ever. There's another picture of Scott and me on our front lawn. I'm wearing his old baseball jersey and a backwards cap while he pulls at the corners of his shirt to show off what it says, a list of inside jokes from his current team. None of it is legible. The average Shoah Foundation interview, according to the organization, runs over two hours in length, with many going even longer. Bubbie's interview makes it past the thirty-five minute mark, but barely.

Watching the tape, I could see why the interviewer struggled so much. She was a stranger to Bubbie, unaware of all her idiosyncrasies. She didn't know how to connect with her, how to corral her in conversation. They shared no rapport. The specifics of Bubbie's delivery, her missteps and omissions, her jumbled sense of time, flew by the woman uncaught and unexamined. Follow-up questions did not help. Bubbie said what she wanted to say, and at the speed she wanted to say it.

In her book *Survivors*, historian Rebecca Clifford explains, "Every interview is a story: a performance of the self and its past for a particular audience... Child survivors, like all people, shape their stories to fit the expectations of their listeners."[23] I recognized this in Bubbie's Shoah Foundation interview. She was hyper-aware of her audience, their goals and intentions, the curve of a narrative arc. Recalling survival is not the same as survival itself. Remembrance has its own set of stakes. Amid the stress and pressure, the flood of old feelings and visceral trauma, Bubbie could not handle the onslaught of questions, the way the interviewer insisted on a certain order, a certain structure, beginning, middle, and end, the way she expected and expected and expected, but did not, could not, understand.

After watching the interview, I knew I was not so different from the blonde woman in the tape. Despite knowing Bubbie my whole life, I could not always keep up with her, with what she could handle and what she couldn't. Our conversations were riddled with confusion, the same as her Shoah Foundation interview nearly twenty years earlier. Bubbie mixed up important details, hopped around in time and misinterpreted my questions. She repeated herself again and again, keeping her phrasing the same every time—in places that made sense and in places that didn't. She was trying to steer me as much as she could, to help me see what she was seeing, but I had a different vantage point. I had the distance she could never possibly possess, both a wider lens and a hunger for detail. She hungered only for it to be over.

When I asked Bubbie for a specific description, what the mandated concentration camp dress was made out of or how it felt, she told me it was gray. When I asked her about events that happened after the war, a particular path she chose or move she made, she waved me off, telling me it wasn't important. "You don't have to write that," she said, her face twisted in distaste. She could not understand why I asked about something so disconnected, so specific and small. For the most part, these details were not anything she planned on telling me.

In trying to trace the line between Bubbie's past and present, I kept tripping over a separate line, the one between the two of us. We saw things so differently. From her point of view, my questions looked in all the wrong places. Her story was not about the courageous things she did during the war or the life she went on to lead after, but about other people. It was about what they did, their cruelty and violence, the terror they were capable of carrying out. That was what was unbelievable to her. But I was more interested in Bubbie. I wanted to consider her, the girl she was, the woman she became, and the hurt she carried. I wanted to know how survival had changed her, had changed everything.

I had set out to invent a language, to build a bridge, hoping Bubbie would lay her words out like sun-dried bricks. Bricks are stable, unmoving objects, easy to hold in one hand. Language, however, refuses such stasis. It is too alive, bending, blooming, breaking into branches, stretching into snaky green sprouts. For us to connect, we would need more than words, more than the straight smooth line. We were on opposite riverbanks, waving, wondering: What now?

Perhaps I was so focused on remembering that I forgot about forgetting, what it had to offer. Forgetting could be a balm, could make space where one needed it most. Like a deep inhale, it could bring in new air. But forgetting is scary to a granddaughter of a genocide survivor, scary in a world that contains denial and algorithms that promote it, ideas of supremacy and division pouring in from the shadows. Online, I saw old tropes take new forms: memes, posts, threads, tweets. The word "globalists." Replacement theory. Space lasers. Someone wrote *88* on a neighbor's window and I sadly knew what it meant. I wrote as much as I could, stacking words into sentences and sentences into paragraphs, but I couldn't remember my way through.

In the spring of 1969, Golda and Benti were busy. Their daughter Hedi, then twenty years old, had gotten engaged. They were thrilled. The future unfurled in front of them, happiness on the horizon. Golda helped her daughter with dress shopping while Benti organized the reception. Everyone was working on something. Two weeks before the big day, while preparations were still being finalized and details confirmed, the family's first out-of-town guest arrived. She came from Israel and she came alone.

Blimchu had never met any of her sister's children before, but flew in regardless to see the eldest one get married. On the day she arrived, Benti and Golda drove to the airport to pick her up—only it wasn't the airport in Detroit. Benti had purchased the tickets for Blimchu's flight since she couldn't afford it on her own. Only he also couldn't afford much. The flight landed in New York City, nearly 650 miles away. Golda and Benti spent hours on the road to get there, Benti doing all the driving. Golda didn't have her own license. No one had ever taken the time to teach her how to drive, including her husband who drove for a living.

When the plane landed, Blimchu was terrified. She thought she'd never find her sister in such a large, cavernous place, thousands of people rushing about, trying to catch their flights. But Golda spotted her right away. Blimchu wore her wavy brown hair short, a pair of glasses hanging off the bridge of her nose. Her skin was tan from living in warmer climes, the ceaseless sun of central Israel. The sisters hugged one another, arms wrapped tight, chatting in the same swift tongue they'd used as little girls.

Blimchu's arrival in New York marked her first and only visit to the United States. She stayed for six weeks, and remained anxious for most of it. She didn't like the States. For one, she couldn't speak any English and was unable to make sense of her surroundings. The suburbs of Detroit looked nothing like the kibbutz. There was nowhere to walk to from her sister's house, so she didn't go anywhere. She sat on the couch while Golda and Benti were at work all day. When the kids came home from school, she stayed where she was, unable to communicate with her English-speaking nieces and nephew. To them, their aunt seemed icy, a silent presence perched on the living room sofa. At Hedi's wedding, Blimchu joined the festivities but more in body than spirit. She did not know the people around her nor did she trust them. She did not get their jokes. Being in the United States was outside her element and she felt deeply, deeply uncomfortable.

After Hedi's wedding, Golda and Blimchu were finally able to catch up. They did so at night, once Golda's shifts at the factory were done for the day. More often than not, they ended up in the kitchen. Blimchu showed her little sister how to make mayonnaise from scratch, as well as several new cookie recipes she'd learned in Israel. She worked as a professional cook there and was exceptionally talented. While their hands kneaded and stirred, they talked about their children and husbands, their everyday lives, but more than that, they remembered their old town of Sighet and all the faces they lost—their beloved parents, their grandparents, their siblings, older and younger. Their losses had become their last commonality, the rest of their lives so markedly different. Blimchu returned to Israel glad to have seen her sister, but relieved to go home. She left as alert and uneasy as ever.

Golda, however, was none of those things. She had become a spring, a gale-force wind of a woman. When her children faltered, she lifted them up. When they succeeded, she bragged to whoever was nearby, whoever was standing in earshot. When her youngest daughter wanted to attend medical school, she convinced her husband to let her go, though he was staunchly against the idea. Whenever something needed to get done, she found a way to do it. She gave so frequently, cooked and cared so much, that she always had someone she could turn to when she needed help. Responsibility was brought to her life in spades and she met it head-on.

Three years later, after a lifetime of not knowing how, Golda decided she was going to learn how to drive. She was done asking for rides. She recruited Hedi, who was then pregnant with her first child, to be her teacher. The two (and a half) women racked up fifty hours on the road together, practicing turns, signals, and stops. It was enough to qualify Golda for the state driver's exam. At the DMV, the administrators granted her an oral exam instead of the usual written one. They asked her question after question, and she answered, passing on her first try. She passed the vision screening and driving test too. At age forty-two, Golda earned her Michigan driver's license and with it, a freedom she had never known before. She was elated.

And so she went, picking herself up and everyone else with her. She loved to give, a reminder that she could now. She had something to offer the world. Not just offer, but push. Insist. Should someone be hungry, she'd fix them a warm meal on the spot. It didn't matter who it was. Often, it didn't even matter if they were hungry. Roasted chicken, potato latkes, a platter of crescent roll cookies for dessert. She'd dole out her sweet, buttery treats, happily taking clean plates and compliments in return. She loved making something from nothing, taking care of those around her. Doing so became even easier with her driver's license in hand. She made chicken soup when friends got sick, drove to their houses, visited distant relatives, helped run errands, dropped off baked goods for special occasions. She was not like her husband and she was not like her sister. Golda was open to the world around her, open and generous and driven. Illiteracy could not stop her. The orphan, the refugee, had made herself a family and a career, creating a life she could finally call her own.

TWENTY

— How did you guys decide to move to the United States?

— We figured the kids had to go to college and from Windsor to college here was a lot. Not only transportation, sign up too. He didn't want to move to Detroit. He wanted to go to Chicago, he wanted to go to California. He didn't know what he wanted. I let him do what he wanted and we ended up in Detroit. Nobody can tell him nothing, you know? Only what he wanted to do, I let him do.

— Did you get a job in the United States?

— Me?

— Yeah.

— Wherever I went, they wanted me. To be in the restaurant, I was sewing, doing something. He went to ask for a job. *I have a job for your wife.* And he was so jealous, it bothered him so much. That's what happened, again and again. So I worked a couple days, I said, *I can't do that. I have the kids home. I can't leave the kids at home.* Later on I got the job at General Motors. That's what helped. Gail was seven year old, I had a job at General Motors. I was there till I was sixty-five years old. That's why I have a good pension. I have to be there to have the medical for the kids, even for Hedi's kids I had medical. Takes a lot. Eye doctor, dentist, everything. Hedi went back to school to become a nurse. And she kept on going to become more, you know. I bought her a car, I bought Becky a car, so they can come and go to school. I did what I could. Here, you want some nuts?

— No, I'm good.

— Why not?

— Aren't we going to have dessert later?

— Yeah, but you can have it now.

— I need more space for dessert, less space for nuts.

— Unbelievable. Bothered you what I went through.

— Yeah.

— Unbelievable. Yeah.

— What was your happiest memory?

— Happiest memory? When I had my baby in my hand.

— Hedi?

— Hedi, all my kids. When I'm done with it. That was an accomplishment to me, to me. Always make parties for them, birthday parties. I go with them, here and there, the birthday parties.

— You guys started with so little, it's amazing how much…

— I accomplished.

— Yes, accomplished.

— Can you imagine? I had nothing.

— I can't imagine.

— I'm lucky that wherever I went, people liked me. He did what he can to prepare, to fix, to do. You know.

— Bubbie, is there anything that scares you?

— Scare me? It's scary because I haven't got the education I want. I can't read, I can't do nothing. I really wanted to. It doesn't go in my head. I read a little bit and I go back, I don't know nothing. Your mother noticed that. She kept pushing me all the time, with teachers to learn, to do, practice, do this. Finally one guy told her, *Listen. She can never comprehend what they try to teach her. She reaches one and that's it. She tries again, she cannot do. Doesn't know.*

— But you know this.

— Know this? I can talk!

— But I mean, you've… you're very smart. You've done all these real estate deals, you've always found your way. You have all these different skills. You're self-taught in cooking and sewing and…

— I learn by myself. I never knew how to sew. The first time I made a dress was for Hedi and Hedi's cousin. Then I made another one, came out perfectly. I was sewing in the factories, leather seats. I said if I can do that, why can't I do this? Didn't even know how to run the machine. I learn that.

— You're very gutsy.

— Yeah, I don't give up. I try.

TWENTY-ONE

As a kid, I had wild teeth, each with its own sense of direction. They crowded, shifted and jutted out. I played with them non-stop, testing their wobbliness with my tongue. I was too timid to ever tug too hard, but too curious not to wiggle them incessantly. The landscape of my mouth fascinated me, how quickly it could change. In third grade, while walking home from school one day, I was wiggling a particularly loose tooth with my tongue when I spotted a large white box sitting on our porch. I ran to the door tongue to tooth, the taste metallic.

The box was two feet wide, maybe three, and like most packages that weren't addressed to me, it excited me right away. My dad told me I had to wait for my mom to open it, so when she got home from work that night, I greeted her at the garage door.

"We got a package!" I announced.

She set her bags down and we hauled the box onto the dining room table. I watched as she slid a box-cutter through the tape, pulling the flaps open. I peeked over the cardboard's edge. The box was full, not an inch of wasted space.

Inside was Hooked on Phonics, a popular reading comprehension program. It was designed to help kids overcome the challenges of learning how to read. I saw commercials for it on TV all the time, ads that featured worried parents and kids with lisps declaring, "Hooked on Phonics worked for me!" My favorite TV channels played the ads over and over, updating them every year or so with new kids, new buzz cuts and buckteeth, new parents full of relief.

My mom carried the box down to the basement and pushed it into an unused nook. I knew she hadn't bought it for me. I had learned to read in first grade and now, two years later, I read every night before bed. Whatever I could get my hands on, I read—comic books, fantasies, biographies, novels. School came easily to me, especially language arts. I enjoyed school so much that on days off, if the weather wasn't nice enough for running around outside or collecting grass with our toes, my next-door neighbor and I pretended her basement was a classroom. We alternated between who got to be the teacher and who was the student, crafting elaborate worksheets with math and grammar problems for the other to solve. We wrote our worksheets in squeaky marker, then switched and filled them out in full. When the white box arrived on my family's front porch, I was more than ready. It felt like my big chance, an opportunity to teach for real.

My mom had purchased the program not for Scott or me, but for her mom. Peering into the box of books, I didn't wonder why Bubbie hadn't learned to read or what obstacles must have stood in her way. I only wanted to help. Without a single thought more, I appointed myself as Bubbie's personal reading instructor. I couldn't wait to teach her to read.

My family lived in a suburb outside Chicago, about five hours from our extended family in Michigan. It was too long a drive for Bubbie to do by herself, so she came by train. With her, she brought two pieces of luggage—a large suitcase for her clothes, and a cooler of the same size packed full of food. She brought chicken, blintzes, onion rolls, pastry dough and other baked goods, both bought and made. "She knows we have food in Chicago, right?" my dad said, more than once.

For our first lesson together, I went into the basement and picked out three books from the white box. They were slim books, easy to thumb through. Every block of text was paired up with a colorful illustration, showy and bright. I laid the books out on our dining room table for her to choose. Without glancing, Bubbie grabbed the one closest to her. We sat side by side at the table, our chairs unusually close. I watched as she put on her glasses, peeled back the front cover and paused to clear her throat. Slowly, she started sounding out the words.

As I listened to Bubbie read aloud, I felt some amazement at how quickly the words came to me, how much progress I had made since first grade. I viewed the words on the page as I view them now—not as a series of shapes or squiggles, but tidy cases packed with meaning. W-o-r-d: put together, a complete idea. The process was automatic for me. How badly Bubbie wanted that ease and knowledge, too. She poured all her effort into deciphering those short, crisp words. She worked to identify the letters one at a time, w-o-r-d, stringing them together with sound until they became a familiar object. Word? Letter by letter, line by line, she made her way through the book.

Until she faltered. Bubbie was unable to place one of the words in front of her and so I said it over her shoulder. She repeated it and kept going. A page later, she stumbled again, putting the sounds together in the wrong way. I corrected her pronunciation in a gentle voice, the same one my elementary school teachers used with me. She let my pronunciation stand in for hers, not wanting to try again, and plodded on to the next word, the next sound. I could tell it was slow, exhausting work for her.

Still, she made progress. At one point, she sounded out the word mountain and I chirped with pride. "Mountain! That's such a big word, Bubbie!" She smiled, always happy to see me happy.

Once she reached the last page, she took her glasses off and set them on the dining room table. The book had taken ten minutes to read, if that. I figured we'd read another one, maybe even all three. Maybe I'd go back into the basement and pick out a few more books for her. But Bubbie was tired. "Come," she said, "let's make the cookies. I'll let you roll the dough."

She got up before I could reply. I wanted to keep reading with her, but I didn't know how to pull her back, back to me and the books and the table and the chairs. In the kitchen, I stood across from her and did as she instructed, flattening a mound of dough into an uneven sheet. She smoothed it out for me and started cutting it to make crescent roll cookies. I used the pads of my fingers to roll the slices of dough and she used hers to point out what was neat and what was not. "Beautiful," she said, moving the tidy ones onto a baking sheet. With the rest, she slapped them into a ball and re-rolled a new sheet, a new set of cookies. I watched her hands, how they kneaded and floured and folded. She was so deliberate, so certain in her movements. There was an ease to the motion, a deep comfort. Later, we pulled the crescent rolls out of the oven and set them to cool. They piled up like mountains across the countertop. I couldn't believe how many cookies we had made. The whole kitchen smelled of butter.

On her next trip to Chicago, I tried again, offering to pick out more books from the box. She read a few lines from one, but couldn't finish. Another time, I wrote my own sentences and printed them off from the computer. I cut them into strips of paper to make each one more manageable on its own. My mom found a magnifying glass to help Bubbie see the letters, the way they clustered together. Still, Bubbie struggled to read them aloud, to parse out the sounds from the shapes.

Our reading sessions were neither her first nor her last attempt at attaining some level of literacy. For years, she made progress, then lost it. She could never hold her concentration in one place, never keep her attention steady—a common symptom for people with post-traumatic stress disorder. My mom tried many things to help her learn and Bubbie went along with all of them. She got the basics down—all the letters in the alphabet, the sounds they make, how to write them—but struggled to put it together in a meaningful, lasting way. It embarrassed her, how little she knew, how difficult those tiny letters were to decipher. The answers seemed to run when she reached for them. For Bubbie, reading was like doing a jigsaw puzzle on a slanted table. Either her brain couldn't take the words in, or it simply wouldn't. Were she able to read the story of Sisyphus, I'm sure she would have understood his woe.

No one told me the word illiterate wasn't allowed, but I knew. My parents, brother and relatives never brought the topic up, never used the word themselves. I suspect it wasn't something my family all agreed upon. She had sounded out the word "mountain," hadn't she? How could that be illiteracy? But whether she could read or not, she didn't. She didn't read signs or instructions. She didn't read the newspaper or the bills that came in the mail. It was a fact we all ignored, a truth we hid. Others did not need to know. Watching my family skirt the issue around friends and neighbors taught me how to skirt it, too.

By the time I was in fourth grade, a strange role reversal set in whenever Bubbie and I stepped out of the house together. In public, she became the secret child who did not know what any signs around us said and I became the secret adult who did, and could, explain as needed, quickly and under my breath. If we went out for lunch together, I listed a few items off the menu for her and she picked the first or second thing I said. She then gave me too much money to pay and I got the appropriate change back. We drew as little attention to ourselves as possible, a skill she had long ago mastered, but one I was just picking up. Stealth was new to me.

At home, we fell into our normal selves, our roles unreversed. She taught Scott and me a card trick and let us perform it for her over and over, ever the gracious audience. We played gin rummy and watched TV, the three of us slumped along the couch. *Baywatch* was her favorite show. She also watched *Wheel of Fortune* nearly every day, something I never understood since she couldn't play along or follow what was happening on the board. But I guess in the end she just liked seeing people win.

The only thing we didn't do was read. There were no more books together, no over-the-shoulder correct-ions or shouts of encouragement. Our reading lessons were over. We all surrendered, gradually and without a word, to her not knowing. Shame filled the space where there was potential, where there was hope. We didn't speak of this, but even as a kid, I could feel it. The white box fell under a thick layer of dust in our basement, a mountain of its own.

Bubbie remained unchanged. She was as she had always been: busy, generous, stubborn, kind—and unable to read. She moved through life in the same ways too, using her voice to ask questions, give instructions, and get things done. She learned landmarks in lieu of street signs, relying on her memory to navigate the world around her. She honed her signature, *Golda Indig* in looping cursive letters, for official documents, and pressed the red power button on her TV's remote control when she wanted the news.

But unlike Bubbie, I was entirely changed. I began to see her as different, not better or worse but her own distinct person. She didn't act how the other adults around me acted, nor did she speak how they spoke. She was direct, softening nothing, her accent making it clear she was from somewhere else. She was different. My whole family was different, and I had simply never noticed before. But now, I noticed everything. New teeth grew into my mouth and I kept quiet, watching everyone around me, observing every detail. I learned to listen, to adapt, to be whatever the time or place called for me to be—creative, contained, athletic, astute. Stealth was critical, a matter of survival. An orthodontist glued braces to my teeth and I grew into a smarter, shyer, more careful person. The lessons had been for me.

TWENTY-TWO

Partway through my Florida trip, Bubbie started to get restless from our interviews. I could tell she needed a break from remembering, from reliving all those old, sordid memories. It was draining work for her and nothing she was used to doing. Over dinner, she suggested we go to one of the casinos near her building. (There were multiple options, this being south Florida and all.) She wanted to play the slot machines.

"You'll like the penny slots," she told me, sliding another helping of food onto my plate.

I was not so sure. I liked long novels and sport climbing, getting ice cream with friends and hanging onto my money. Gambling always struck me as more of a reckless activity than a thrilling one. The risk never seemed worth the reward. Still, I knew I couldn't say no. It's not every day that your grandma invites you to go gambling with her. I was here, she was here: we were going to the casino.

I dropped Bubbie off at the front of the building and found a parking spot while she waited for me in the lobby. The place was overwhelming, covering every box on the gambling establishment checklist: fat glowing lights in clashing colors, garish posters, a never-ending patterned carpet, security cameras dotting the ceilings, and rows upon rows of buzzing, glittering, flashing machines. Since it was my first time there, the casino gave me a complimentary $25 card to get started. The lady behind the counter also handed me three shiny strands of Mardi Gras beads in green, purple and gold. I threw the beads around my neck and offered Bubbie my arm. It was time to find the penny slots.

Bubbie wasn't the only one growing restless. The more time we spent together, the more mixed-up I felt. I was lost inside her memories, in the sound and shake of her voice, her meandering narration, the way I asked one question and she answered another. If I thought our interviews were intimate conversations, she thought they were footraces. And she was winning. Her words rushed one another, leaving me tangled in the threads of her testimony. I wanted her to slow down, stay in the moment, offer a little more detail. I never knew what was what.

But misunderstanding one another was a well-established part of our relationship. Sometimes I underestimated Bubbie and she proved me wrong. Other times, I assumed she thought like I did and was mistaken again. Once I told Bubbie a movie I had seen was deep and she asked me what I was saying. I repeated it louder, thinking it was matter of hearing. "It was deep!" I yelled. She scrunched her forehead. "What does that mean?" she asked. I had forgotten. My first language was not the same as hers. All those fairy tales and folk stories she'd told me as a kid, the ones about Bubbie Beitzah and her little ones, the cottage, the skirt, the wolf's pointy fangs, they were translations, words taken from her first language and transposed to her sixth.

No matter what the topic, Bubbie spoke in a non-linear manner, starting one thought and finishing another. She bobbed freely between ideas, times, people, and places. I was the opposite, bound to logic and desperate for clarity. Even my work in advertising was centered around the idea of concise, clear language, easy-to-understand concepts, and copy. I wanted everything to make sense, and got frustrated when it didn't. Perhaps that was why I coveted stories so much. They could serve as maps to the madness all around.

As Bubbie aged, the misunderstandings between us had grown more frequent and more complex. Her ability to recall names and events was beginning to decline. She forgot whether or not she took her medicine, then took two days at once or none at all. She lost things in her condo and blamed others for stealing them, finding them a day or two later in the place where she'd last set them. She couldn't hold as much in her head as she used to be able to, an uncomfortable reality for everyone in my family. She said uh-huh over and over to appease whoever was talking to her, to give the impression that she was following along. But I had to wonder. Hadn't she always said uh-huh a lot? Didn't I get annoyed as a kid when she'd say uh-huh to me even though I hadn't said anything to her? She was never a particularly good listener. And was she ever so great at recalling names and dates? Did they ever matter that much to her?

When I was in middle school, my family took Bubbie bowling. She had never been before, a fact I could not believe at the time. My friends from school threw bowling birthday parties all the time. I knew how to line my feet up, how to hold the ball, place my fingers, sometimes how to get a spare. Bubbie wore a long floral dress to the bowling alley that day, her rental shoes peeking out beneath its bottom hem. When it was her turn to bowl, she squared her shoulders to the pins, locked her feet in place. She winded up and released. I still remember the thud the ball made as it landed halfway down the lane. She didn't know you're supposed to roll a bowling ball, not throw it, and none of us had thought to tell her.

Whenever I spent time with Bubbie, I tried to follow her lead as much as possible, to see where her thinking would take us. Inevitably, she'd say something I didn't understand or I'd say something she didn't get, and we'd start over, try again. I rephrased, reframed, shouted louder, listened closer, and still, always, got lost in the mix. I learned to give short answers to Bubbie's questions so she'd understand me, and ask short questions in return. It was easier that way. Cover as little as possible and maybe it'd click. On phone calls, we stuck to the same reliable subjects, our go-to topics. We discussed the weather and if I was dressing warm enough for it, how Scott was doing, and my parents. We talked about if I was home or not, how I was getting home, when I'd be back. In little loops we went: weather, family, home. I had no idea what it was like to talk about a good book with one's grandma, or discuss current events, or seek an opinion on a personal matter. I called mine to say hello and let her know I was all right. When I did tell her what I was up to, what I did that day or week, I left out places and names, since I doubted she'd retain them anyway. I erased the more complicated edges off my stories, dulling them to their core.

Words didn't just get in her way, but in my way too. I relied on them to express myself and felt lost without. How does one understand without sentences? Without paragraphs? My world was built on them in a way hers was not, and I couldn't figure out how to relate without language as a brace. I never lied to her, but rarely did I offer her the full truth either. It was complex, too messy and hard to explain. Instead, I adjusted to how she thought—or how I thought she thought. I kept the details vague, trying to minimize her concern. Did it work? I had no idea, but in the process, I learned to limit myself, to self-censor as I spoke. I talked on tiptoes. We were close in so many ways, Bubbie and I, but sometimes we could barely connect. Sometimes it was like we didn't know each other at all.

So when Bubbie suggested we go to the casino, I agreed, even though what I really wanted was to talk some more. I wanted to keep digging, to better understand how she survived survival, how she lived with illiteracy. I was determined to learn her story, to hold onto it, preserve it in some way. Perhaps taking some time away from her living room, away from my laptop and its steady green dot of a light, would help things fall into place. Perhaps our communication would slide into a smoother gear. If it took penny slots for us to get there, I was willing to give it a try.

The casino, like most casinos, was laid out like an oversized labyrinth, designed to disorient its mostly elderly players. Bubbie and I managed to find our way to a bank of slot machines against a long black wall. She had refused to take her cane with her again and used my elbow instead. We sat at the slot machines and played, the pre-loaded casino card funding our bets. We weren't at the machines for long before I realized that, although the slot machines had been her idea, she didn't know how to play them. Not really, anyway. She couldn't read any of the labels on the machine, so each button was essentially the same to her. Push something, see what happens. On the side of each slot machine was a cartoonish lever, the physical embodiment of the word *cha-ching!* When I asked her what it did, she shrugged. "I don't know, call for help?"

We played two machines at once, with me adjusting the bets for both. I wasn't sure what I was doing either, but with each round I started to pick up what would sometimes work and what never did. Our winnings went up, then down, then up again. We fell into a rhythm, pressing, waiting, counting. To my own surprise, I kind of liked it. It was fun. We cashed out with $25.09 in our pockets, a nine-cent gain from the original card. Not too shabby for two people pushing buttons at random.

After we collected our winnings at the counter, Bubbie and I started to make our way to the exit, but we couldn't figure out which way to go. Too many things tried to distract us from leaving. There was a singer belting James Taylor in the far corner, harsh-colored lights in every shade imaginable, and distant exit signs that pointed both to the left and the right. We made it to one of these exits, but it was the wrong one, so we rested on a low-slung couch by the door. Bubbie grimaced as she sat. Her knee, replaced a year earlier, was aching; she needed a minute to catch her breath. In and out, she puffed, straining for air. This was more walking than she was used to doing.

When we made it to the correct exit, I told her to wait at one of the benches outside the door so I could get the car and pull it around. I couldn't stand hearing her breathe so heavily, her sighs when she sat. How she would lean against the wall or clutch a chair to keep her balance—it saddened me. She used to be so strong. When I was a kid, I'd sit on her feet and she'd bounce me up and down in the air. Sometimes, she'd hold my hands in hers, but other times she'd let me fly. I'd explode with giggles, going every which way aboard my own personal rocket launcher. Now, I pulled the car through the valet lane to make the walk a little shorter.

Flanking the casino entrance were tall potted plants, stately columns and a couple of benches, both of which were empty. Bubbie wasn't there. She wasn't leaning against the planters or one of the columns either.

I spun in my seat, craning my neck to see around the building, the seatbelt straining against the motion. I didn't see her anywhere. She could barely walk and yet she was missing. Again.

After sweet-talking the attendant into letting me linger in the valet lane, I put the car in park and started walking in small, concentric circles. How could I lose her? How could I lose her again? Only a handful of hours had passed since the mix-up at the hair salon and the "emergency" on the fourth floor. I was as confused as ever, and on the edge of serious worry. Hadn't she been tired and out of breath minutes earlier in the casino? Hadn't she needed to rest, her knee feeling worn out and in pain? I knew her gripping my arm wasn't a figment of my imagination, her pausing to catch herself, body and breath. She had been too tired to go on before, but now, here, when I asked her not to, she had gone on anyway.

I tried to think where she might've gone. Back into the casino? Into another car? Lying in a ditch somewhere?

Finally, I spotted her. Far from the front entrance, along the perimeter of the casino's parking lot, she was holding onto a flimsy metal fence. The wind whipped around her.

"Bubbie," I shouted. "What are you doing? I said I'd pull the car up to the front. By the benches."

"I move here to make it easier for you."

Make it easier? For me? Bubbie was standing near the parking lot's entrance, where we had first driven in, assuming that's where I'd be coming from again. But I had come from the other side, the side where the cars were parked. By trying to make things easier for me, she had made them much more difficult. Her knee ached when she put weight on it, but still she could not bear to sit still and wait, to let me be the one making things easier. I'd been gone for five minutes, if that, to get her car and pull it around to the front of the building.

I never wanted to lose Bubbie, and yet I'd managed to do it twice in one day. Wasn't the whole point of the trip not to lose her? I gave Bubbie my arm and we walked back to the valet lane.

The parking attendant looked over and I gave him a nod, in part to thank him for letting me park illegally and in part to confirm that yes, I did find my missing grandma. I opened the passenger door for Bubbie and helped her step inside. She pulled the seatbelt across her chest and I buckled it in. I did not understand her thinking and knew she did not understand mine. Our trip to the casino had not gone how either one of us planned. But, if nothing else, we could relate to each other's breathless fatigue. That we shared in full.

TWENTY-THREE

One day in 1988, many years after the war and without explanation, my grandfather told my grandma he wanted to see Sighet again. Something inside him told him to go. Golda didn't want to join, at least not right then, and he didn't want to wait, so he bought an airplane ticket on his own. He called his near-lookalike brother Barry and convinced him to come with, offering to buy his airplane ticket too. In no time at all, the men were on their way.

The brothers flew to Europe, going all the way back to their little town off the Tisza River. Benti wanted to see what he could remember there. The men walked around Sighet, noting all that had changed. So many of the people they'd grown up with had died or fled; so few had stayed behind. They visited their parents' gravestones, saying their hellos and goodbyes all at once. For their mother and father to have gravestones at all was a major accomplishment of the brothers' doing. Like so many others, their parents had died in Nazi concentration camps far from home. The stones marked their lives, but not their bodies.

Death was on the minds of many. During the 1980s, a small group of Jewish survivors from the Maramos area, of which Sighet was the capital, decided to write a book to preserve the histories of their once-vibrant towns. Yizkor books, or books of memory, were being created for villages all across Europe, places scarred by war and forever changed by the decimation of their Jewish communities. In the Maramos book, published in Hebrew in 1983, the authors documented the events of the Holocaust as well as details about prewar life, including customs, folklore, and holidays. "It is possible to expand upon certain specific, unique characteristics, indigenous only to the Jews of Marmaros, for example, the atmosphere and the spirit in the town on the High Holidays, the days of penitential prayers, the ten days of repentance, etc. But suffice it to have described several general features in order to be able to have some concept of Jewish life in a world which is no longer and will never again be." [24] The authors also note that the Jews of Marmaros were "by nature very sentimental," which no doubt applied to Benti and his long venture home. (And to me and my writing of this book.)

At some point during their trip, the two brothers got into an argument. About what, no one can say. They fought all the time, I'm told. Was one disagreement really that different from another? They were stubborn men, prone to argument, always getting under one another's skin. The details were rarely deemed relevant.

After their time in Sighet, the brothers flew from Romania to the United Kingdom. By then, Barry was ready for the trip to end. But even on this, the brothers could not agree. Benti felt something inside him tell him not to go. Not yet. Unfortunately, his flight home was coming up, while Barry still had a few more days in the UK. The solution seemed obvious to them. Benti would stay and see London—a city he'd never seen before— while Barry would return home early. The brothers switched plane tickets and passports and Mr. Barry Indig flew home as Mr. Benti Indig. The two men really did look alike.

Meanwhile, Benti toured London alone. What he did all day, I do not know. No one in my family does. What we do know is that when it was time to board Barry's original flight home, Benti was there. He got on the plane. Buckled his seatbelt. The plane took off. After several minutes in the air, he felt something inside again. Only this time it wasn't an abstract longing or a deeply felt sadness. This time it was a myocardial infarction. Somewhere over the Atlantic Ocean, Benti had a heart attack. He seized up, muttering in Yiddish, words no one around him could understand. The flight attendants alerted the pilot; the pilot turned the plane around. By the time they landed back in London, Benti was gone.

That day, my great-aunt Faigu got a phone call in Windsor. It was the airline with the sad news that her husband Barry had died in the middle of his transatlantic flight home. Imagine her surprise, especially when her husband was playing cards with her at their kitchen table, sipping a cup of coffee she'd just made. The men may have been similar in face and name, but they had different wives, and passports from different nations.

My family sorted out the confusion of who was dead and who was alive, who was here and who was there. They managed to arrange my grandfather's return, with a proper funeral to follow. Everyone gathered at the cemetery in Windsor for his burial—my grandma, my great-aunt, her still-alive husband, their children, their friends—with one notable exception. Bubbie had barred my mom from attending. It was bad luck, she insisted, mixing life and death like that. At the time of my grandfather's funeral, my mom was nearing the end of her third trimester; her belly was round and low. She was pregnant with a daughter, the last of the grandchildren—a.k.a. me. I wouldn't get a chance to meet my grandfather, but I'd meet Bubbie right away. I'd meet her in more chaos, the stream having no end.

After I was born in a car in Bubbie's driveway, my parents named me Brooke, in honor of my late grandfather. Naming after the deceased, even in first initial only, is a common practice in Judaism. It is meant to commemorate the person who died, to honor them and keep their memory alive. Partway through my trip to Florida, so many years later, Bubbie revealed to me an important note about this fact. It was a small piece of information, a minor detail. And I couldn't believe it. Benti was not his real name. My whole life, I'd had no idea.

Though I'd never met my mom's dad, I was confident I knew his name. I was his namesake after all. Benti was the Eastern European version of the name, or so I thought, with Ben being the more Westernized version. Ben's Coffee Shop, right? In downtown Windsor, Canada? But in fact, the name Benti had been Westernized too. His real name was Benczi (pronounced Ben-see). I had no idea. From talking with Bubbie, I also discovered that his lookalike brother Barry was not actually named Barry. His real name was Mendel, a fact I could not wrap my head around.

She had more to share with me. While sitting with Bubbie in her living room, I discovered she was full of these small, unassuming details, details that turned out to be quite monumental, at least to me. Per her recollections, there was more to say about my grandfather's story, more to his unexpected end. I was amazed by how much she had never told me until I asked. Was that all it took?

Right before he left for Romania, my grandfather set aside ten thousand dollars. This was no small amount for him. He told his wife the money was meant to cover his funeral and whatever death-related expenses might one day come up. Did he somehow know he was about to die? Did he sense it? He sold his taxicab, his sole source of income, and had already reserved a double-plot at a Jewish cemetery in Canada for him and his wife, part of a larger family special he went in on with his brothers. Perhaps he was a good planner, or one prone to thinking through worst-case scenarios. He certainly went through a lot of worst-case scenarios in his life and I'm sure ten thousand dollars would've come in handy. Perhaps his past health issues had been weighing on his mind. His in-air heart attack had not been the first cardiac event he'd experienced. Maybe my grandfather had a premonition that he was going to die soon. Or maybe not. It could have been something else altogether, something he sought out, something he wanted. Stay with me—it's not a totally outrageous idea. Only five years earlier, his depression had been taking him to increasingly dark places. He was having suicidal thoughts, a fact I know because he asked my mom, a third-year med school student at the time, how he should go about doing it, how he should end his life. She answered him with a river of tears. Eventually she was able to get her dad the mental healthcare he needed, and he was able to live on to meet three more grandchildren he never would have met otherwise, including my brother Scott. He adored his grandkids and would buy cases of candy bars as treats for their visits, eager to spoil them with love and sugar. He was softer in their presence, able to access a tenderheartedness he could not manage with the rest of his family. In the end, he got to know and hold all of his grandchildren, save for one.

Looking back at this man I never met, whose real name I only recently learned, I wondered about the final weeks of his life. Maybe he sensed his death was coming, or maybe he willed it to happen. Maybe it was a strange coincidence, the unusual cross-occurrence of thorough end-of-life planning, weirdly poetic timing, and cardiac arrest at mile-high heights. Only he wasn't even supposed to be on that flight, having extended the excursion at the very last minute. What was he feeling the day he was supposed to fly home? Was he not ready to return? Why? Did he not want to go home? I realize a man can't know he is going to have a heart attack in several days and stall for time. He can't will his heart to stop once the seatbelt sign turns off. Yet he'd made so many arrangements to make his death easier on everyone that I couldn't help but consider the timing of it all. What had been running through his mind? What made him want to see his parents' graves, to say his goodbyes right then? He was sixty-five years old when his heart gave way.

I asked Bubbie what she made of all this strange timing and coincidence, but she couldn't track with my thinking. She had been more shocked than anyone when my grandfather died. While he was out of town, she had gotten new carpeting installed throughout their house as a nice surprise for him. (This strikes me as a pretty weak surprise, but such is the difference between my grandma and me.) Though they were husband and wife and still caring for one another, they could not read each other very well. Bubbie, for one, could never see the fog that the war had put her husband in, could never understand how it stiffened his muscles and spirit. How the trauma pressed against his chest like a case of lead. It had had the opposite effect on her, adding a sense of urgency to all her actions, like wind powering a turbine. It taught her how to move, how to keep moving, how to never stop moving. It taught her how to solve problems, and how to make more when there were none left in the queue. She was wholly different from her husband. Their age gap had meant that she'd been a child during the war—still growing in mind and body, still learning how to be—while he had been an adult. In her most formative years, war was her teacher. In his most formative years, he'd had a teacher.

The two spent their time together yelling, clashing on nearly every issue. And yet, even as they fought and flared, a marriage on the fritz, she never untied herself from him, this man who promised to take her dancing and never did. But then again, did he not waltz her out of a bruised and battered Europe, and on to a life of safety and shelter? Did he not give her family when she'd had none? They had been partners from postwar Sighet on: to small-town Germany outside the displaced persons camp; to parenthood; to resettlement and English as a Second Language courses; to the lunch-and-coffee scene in downtown Windsor; to the car-filled suburbs of Detroit, Michigan. They never stopped being one another's complement, their tether from the old world to the new. They lived in the same places and faced the same scarcities. They struggled with money, and the lack of it, together. New technology puzzled them both, and new trends passed them by in equal stride. They were partners in survival. Though my grandfather was well prepared for his death, my grandma had not seen it coming.

And so, on that hot June night when I was born, it was this newly widowed version of Bubbie that I met. She had been married since she was seventeen years old and now, at fifty-seven, she found herself on her own for the first time in a long time. She could take her life in any direction she so chose, any route she wanted. She had never been in a position like this before, one of open doors. From all her time working in the auto factory, she had attained relative financial stability, a good grasp on the English language and a bevy of friends from all over the world. The possibilities were boundless, like nothing she'd confronted before.

Without realizing it, Golda decided to follow in her mother Henia's footsteps. After becoming a widow, she did not remarry despite having several interested suitors. She dated one of them for two decades, but never fully committed to him, choosing instead to focus her time on her family. She wanted to provide for her children and their kids too, to take care of them above all else.

To do so, Bubbie continued to work at General Motors, an exhausting job but one that came with a reliable paycheck and solid health insurance. She woke up at four in the morning to go to the auto plant. Her shift didn't start until seven, but she went in early to sell jewelry on the side. She was always hustling, always trying to deliver. She wore her goods on her hands so that no one would steal them from her car. When someone complimented her on a piece, she'd try to sell it to them on the fly. She was scrappy. She extended credit to her co-workers when they couldn't get it elsewhere, keeping tracking of what kind of jewelry they liked and how much they owed. She gave others opportunities while creating her own.

Around this time, Golda encouraged her daughter Hedi to end her crumbling marriage. Things were not going well. She offered for Hedi and her three children to move in with her—a chance for a fresh start. My aunt took her up on it.

Golda sold the two small homes she owned, including the one whose driveway I was born in. In their place, she bought a large house in a good school district for Hedi's children. The pool in the backyard was an unplanned bonus. Yellow coneflowers grew up to Golda's hips, a border of brilliant color wrapping around the yard, the lushness its own kind of reward. She watered the garden daily, inviting friends over to swim as much as she could.

After living in the house for several years, Golda aged into her pension at General Motors. She could finally retire. Her children threw her a party to celebrate, filling the house with food, family and friends. They got her a sheet cake with her picture printed on the top, crisp scripted letters wishing her a happy retirement in yellow frosting. I helped her blow out the candles. But despite all the festivities, the thirty-one years in the factory and the party to call it a wrap, Golda didn't take retirement as a cue to slow down. She stuck to her usual ways: cleaning the house, watering the garden, paying the bills, cooking the meals, supporting her family, everything as she'd always done it before. She stayed active, taking care of everyone and everything she could (including, unknowingly, her grandson's marijuana plant in the basement).

Only when my cousins all graduated from high school and moved on to college and the army, only then did Bubbie start to move on too. She sold the house with the pool and bought other properties, both in Michigan and Florida, becoming a snowbird for a short while. She loved the warm weather in south Florida, the breeze off the rich-blue ocean. Eventually, she made herself into a full-time resident. She bounced between a few buildings between Boca Raton and Miami until settling into the penthouse unit with the off-white living room and the balcony that pointed west.

Lying on the couch in that living room, I was struck by how much my family didn't know because so few had lived to tell us, and how much we did know because Bubbie had. She was our looking glass on time gone by, a rope to the painful, strange, honest, and petty details of family history that would otherwise be lost to time. There were so many. She connected my family to a trove of these nearly forgotten stories, almost-lost identities, cultures, customs, and places. She filled in gaps we didn't know were there, gaps in our own selves. She helped us remember what had been lost and what had been taken, not by time or chance, but by calculated acts of terror. The loss was staggering, a disappeared world. Bubbie connected us to this history, seismic in scale, agonizing in detail, and all the family truths it obscured.

Bubbie also connected me, more specifically, to my grandfather. She connected me to the name I wear in his memory and reminded me, once and for all, what that name was. Benczi, the man who wanted nothing more than to see his hometown one more time, to see that his parents were honored despite their horrific deaths. Benczi, who fled on a ship, who died on a plane, who craved stability and tradition most of all. His head was always turned in that direction, turned toward the past. Perhaps his return to Sighet brought him a sense of finality, both for his parents and himself, a sense that he could let his heavy heart rest. I can't help but hope.

TWENTY-FOUR

On our last full day together, Bubbie got a delivery from a local Jewish organization that sent meals to Holocaust survivors once a month. My mom had registered her for the program to give her a break from cooking, especially now that she didn't need to feed anyone but herself. Bubbie didn't seem to get the memo, or care to. When she told me she wanted to stop by a friend's place down the street, I didn't give it much thought. I grabbed the car keys and out we went.

In her friend's apartment building, Bubbie led us down a drab hallway to a dark brown door. She knocked twice. When her friend answered, Bubbie stretched out her hands, offering the woman the donated meal, so she could have it instead. The woman, slightly hunched and slow moving, accepted the food and invited us in to sit and stay for a while. Bubbie told her we couldn't. "Too busy," she said. On the way back to the lobby, I asked Bubbie why she'd said that, why she didn't want to spend a little time with her friend. She explained. The lady talked too much.

I may have wanted more understanding, but that was not something Bubbie could give me. No matter how I tried, how I analyzed and studied and listened and learned, I would have to accept that some things contradict. Some people receive in order to give. Some people give in order to move, to avoid the stiffness of an old armchair, an aging body, a brutal past. We may not have been able to talk about everything, but we were able to share it, to observe and help and make and do. I was exactly what Bubbie had hoped for: company for the road.

Despite all the errands we had already run, there was still one more place she wanted to go. I drove and Bubbie navigated. Every day of my trip had been like this, me heeding to her whims, following them down busy streets and strip malls, making sudden turns, trying to be generous but feeling drained instead. Our every move was dictated by what she wanted to do, her endless and inefficient errands around town. Often I didn't know where we were going until after we arrived.

I thought our day was winding down when she told me to turn left, back towards the condo. But no. A left turn here and a right turn there led us not to her building, but a prime parking spot in front of the grocery store. We had already gone to Publix several times, intentionally and not, so I didn't know why we were back again, buying more food when we had just given a free meal away.

Soon enough, I'd find out. Apparently Elizabeth, the neighbor with an ear for gossip, also had an eye for bargains. She regularly wrote down weekly grocery specials on an index card for Bubbie, who stuffed the card in her purse, ready to go should she find a ride to the store. Maybe she remembered the card in the moment, or maybe she'd had this trip in mind all along. I had no idea. I was merely the driver.

Once we were inside the store, Bubbie grabbed a shopping cart and pushed it toward the first worker she saw. She handed him the card with Elizabeth's hand-written notes. There was something quite kind about writing down discounts for a neighbor and something quite trusting about getting them without knowing what they were for. A part of me wondered why Bubbie hadn't asked me to help, to read the items and find them in the store, but I figured this was how she usually did it. This was her way.

"I want these," she told the worker. It didn't bother her that she didn't know the specifics. A good deal was a good deal.

"Sure thing, ma'am," the man replied. "Follow me."

The polo-shirted grocery worker turned on his heel and led us through the store, weaving between awkward food stands and octogenarians. There were more people with walkers there than without. We stayed close behind the worker, following his steps, the three of us hunters on a bargain food item chase.

When he got to the freezer section, the man turned down one of the aisles and began to probe more closely. Apparently we were shopping for boxed frozen dinners. He slowed down to scan the shelves and find the item, the first from Elizabeth's list. Bubbie, who had left her cane at home again, was pushing a bulky cart behind him, leaning forward. She rammed full force into the man. Bam.

The worker didn't fall, but he did bend down and grab his ankles. He looked hurt. He turned to me with big eyes and I turned to her.

"Bubbie! You hit him," I said.

"Eh," she grinned. "He doesn't need his legs."

The man and I shared half a moment of stunned silence then busted into laughter. What a thing to say! No apology, no explanation, no hint of remorse, just a perfectly formed joke. And great delivery, too. The hurt in the man's face, the rudeness of the blow—it all melted away.

The three of us kept shopping as if a minor assault in the frozen food aisle never happened. So this is how she does it, I thought. This is how it happens. For a moment, I had run out of frustration, out of fatigue. It was funny. She'd made herself a problem and she'd solved it. What an impulse. It was as simple as that, reckless and elegant all at once. What I couldn't learn from language, from direct expression, I'd have to learn from action, from the subtleties of patterns that love to repeat.

TWENTY-FIVE

— So, if I don't know what to do, what advice do you have for me?

— I don't know. Type it out and that's it. What can you do? Is it enough to make a book with that? A story?

— Yeah.

— Figure it out. Maybe you can sell it. Try and see. What happened to a young child from the concentration camp. How much she went through. Little by little, you figure out how to do it.

— OK. That's good.

— Yeah? Put it all on one paper and you know what to do. It comes to you in time, you know how to do.

— What do you want people to take away from it?

— Take away?

— What should other people take away from your story?

— They can only listen. What can you take away?

TWENTY-SIX

I love that exchange. I had been trying to ask for words of wisdom in a general sense, curious how her wartime experiences might influence the life advice she'd have for me. She misunderstood and gave me writing advice instead. Bubbie, who never learned to read, who never scrawled more than a mailing address on a box of baked goods, assumed I was asking for her take on how to draft a book, and doled it out without an ounce of hesitation. And what's amazing to me is how good her advice is, how sound. It solves all the things I get stuck on, both in my writing and in life. Put it down and you'll know what to do. If you don't, give it time. It will come. It will come, it will come, it will come.

Since age six, Golda has been an immigrant; since age fourteen, an orphan and survivor of the Holocaust. She is an outsider in every way, a renegade and refugee. She outlived her parents, her husband, her neighbors, her siblings, her relatives and most of her friends. She saw life through war and disease, marriage and children, and more. When she was seventy-four years old, she was diagnosed with breast cancer and underwent radiation therapy and a double mastectomy. She lost her dyed dark-brown locks, covering her head with brightly colored scarves and short permed wigs. When the cancer was in remission and she was clear of its cells, she grew her hair back in full, deciding that after all that, after all those years spent otherwise, she was actually a blonde at heart. She's been blonde ever since.

During our conversations in Florida, Bubbie told me that throughout her life she often felt she had no one she could to talk to. No one she could share her feelings with, the trauma that lurked inside. She was too busy trying to put food on the table. She had money to think about, the kids, the house, the holidays, and a thousand other things too. For Bubbie to share her story, she had to wait. She had to wait until the bills were paid, mouths fed, children schooled and grown. The grandkids, too. She took care of everybody and everything. To share her story, she had to wait for someone to come along and listen. Someone who could keep up, or try to keep up, someone who could record her words and uncover the rest. She had to wait for that person to finish school, develop their chops. She had to wait for them to say yes, buy an airplane ticket, catch a shuttle van, set their laptop up on a dining room chair and say, "OK, it's recording."

On the last day of my trip, as I was packing my bag for the flight home, Bubbie gave me a gift. As precious as this may sound, it wasn't. She liked playing matchmaker between people and objects. She would offer me something—never wrapped, never personalized in any way—and when I passed on the object, offer it to my cousin or my aunt or an acquaintance she barely knew, until the item moved from her collection to theirs. She was always trying to give people things. It was a hobby for her, the way finding nice ways to say no had become for me. She offered me earrings although my ears aren't pierced—something she also offered to fix on multiple occasions, using a sewing needle, ice cube, and potato. (I always passed.) She offered me stretchy camisoles, glass figurines and used umbrellas. She offered me framed photos straight off her shelves, food from her fridge, necklaces, charm bracelets, ornate gold brooches. (Can you tell I'm not a brooch person?) She offered me candy bars from Israel and Canada, Kahlúa-filled chocolates, flip flops, paper-thin scarves, metal candlesticks and unflattering dresses. I tried to reply to her as politely and firmly as possible: no, that's so generous, no thank you, no room, no, not today, no thanks, not my style, no that's all right, no, I can't, no, no, it won't fit, please no, no.

On this particular day, she handed me a fleece-like blanket in a creamy shade of ivory. It was rich as fur, but fake as veneers. I felt both sides, plush and silky to the touch. I softened under its weight. It was incredibly thick, soothing even. I couldn't quite believe it, but for the first time, I liked one of Bubbie's random gifts. I decided to keep it.

I thanked her and began rearranging everything in my bag to make room for the blanket. There wasn't much space for it, folded, rolled, stuffed or otherwise. Bubbie lay on the couch beside me and watched as I played a complicated game of Tetris with all my belongings. I took items out of my duffel, moved them around, rolled them up and scrunched them down. I was determined to fit everything in.

Through a series of shifts and shuffles, I managed to squeeze the blanket into my bag. Only now the zipper would not budge. I tried sitting on my bag to make it a little smaller. I pressed it down and pushed the sides in with my knees. I stomped on it. The zipper did not move. I put on another shirt to make more room. Once I managed to zip my bag shut, I would leave for the Fort Lauderdale airport and we would both go back to our regularly programmed lives. I would return to winter and work, and Bubbie would return to life without company. We'd both go back to the routine of long-distance phone calls every other week or so, calls that would last two or three minutes at most. Four if we were really feeling chatty. Zero if she meant to call someone else.

I used my shin to press the blanket down into the duffel bag. The zipper closed halfway, then unzipped itself completely.

With one more shove and squeeze, I got my bag to close with the fake fleece blanket tucked inside. As I did so, Bubbie remembered something. She got up from the couch and walked to the back of her closet. The air-conditioning kicked up a notch, whirring a little louder.

"It comes with a matching bear!" she shouted over it.

From her closet, she presented me with a teddy bear in the same creamy shade of ivory fake fur. It was soft and sweet-looking and I did not want it. Stuffed animals did not appeal to me, not since I was in elementary school. I wondered what kind of blankets came with matching teddy bears, but not for long.

"No room," I half-yelled over the A/C. Then, a bit nicer, "It won't fit in my bag. No thank you, Bubbie."

She shrugged, unable to push the issue. She saw how stuffed my duffel bag was, the pull on the seams. It looked like it might burst at any moment. "OK," she said, "I find someone else."

Bubbie and I could not relate to one another, not really. Our lives were too different. So much separated us: geography, time, language, education, experience, skills, hobbies, general hearing ability. What I couldn't understand is what she thought about all those days she was walking through a frozen German countryside with fighter planes droning above her and shoes that could barely stay together underneath. Was it possible for someone to think nothing at all? To be so numb to the world around them that they can walk and walk and walk and not think a single thought? I only ever thought or overthought, so I could not say. And I could not fathom how she felt on her wedding day when no one was there to bear witness but her one aunt and sister. She had been part of such a large, connected family, overflowing with siblings, cousins, uncles and aunts, almost none of whom would ever meet her spouse. And how, I wondered, did she feel so many years later when she got the news that her husband had died, the man she'd fought with endlessly, but who gave her three children and a cobbled-together sense of place in the world? They had been partners for the majority of their lives, but bitter, volatile ones, ones with grudges and the words to express them in multiple languages. I couldn't grasp how she navigated such a tenuous union, how she kept her balance for forty years, then kept it well past then too, finding ways to thrive without his help. Even now, I couldn't imagine how she must feel with her mind and body starting to fade, her knees aching so intensely, but her spirit as feisty and restless as ever. She was the same on-the-go machine she'd always been, giving and receiving, solving problems, making more, despite having slowed down with age, too. She lost her breath when she crossed a room, but still, she crossed many rooms and fed many people. Her days were both active and slow, easy and stressed. She was full of contradictions like these and more, contradictions I could barely make sense of. I tried, the copywriter in me so badly wanting to put some rhythm to the constant banging drums, but I couldn't do it. I couldn't wrap my head around all her choices, overlapping and ever-changing as they were. The world looked immensely different from our vantage points.

What I could understand is why Bubbie gave so much. She gave and gave and gave some more. She gave unusual gifts and phenomenal meals, and had for many years. Her generosity was relentless. I understood the power she found in giving, in having people lean on you, in having them need you. How they sit down. How they stay. Or if they leave, how they return, time and time again. It was so rare for her to see someone leave in her childhood and come back unscathed, come back at all. In the camps, she was often alone, in hiding, her stomach a field of emptiness. Now, decades later and on another continent, none of that was the case and she wasted no time in giving what she could, taking care of those around her, socializing and cooking, feeding loved ones without limit. I understood why she gave, why she needed to feel that power, the power to draw people to your table and make them full. It's the feeling of being full yourself. How elusive that feeling can be.

For Bubbie, this paradox, this sense of understanding and misunderstanding, knowing and not knowing, was as strong for her as it was for me. She didn't know what I did all day at work. What the computers had to do with the meetings, and the meetings with the writing. She didn't understand why I climbed, why I chose to leave the shelter of perfectly flat ground. Traveling to Kentucky because they have good rock there didn't make a lick of sense to her. And she didn't get why I was shy in some contexts but not in others, how I modulated my personality both consciously and not. She modulated nothing. Even this word modulate—which I have now used in the last three sentences—is unfamiliar to her. So many of my words, my ideas and worries, my unfettered thoughts, they seem odd to her. Foreign even. From being persecuted and needing to flee to finally being able to do so, Bubbie got grandchildren who are nothing like her, grandchildren she cannot relate to. Ambitious, goofy, shortsighted American grandchildren. She cannot figure us out. The distance between us, like so much else, is a legacy of the war and persecution, the impact of displacement. Yet, in a strange way, it is also a marker of her success. She tried to escape and did. She wanted our lives to be different from hers and they are, an urgent correction. The distance grew into a protective barrier, an intentional act. I was a puzzle to her because of it.

But sometimes, more than anyone else, my grandma did understand me. She saw me as I was. Like when I told her in a quiet voice over the phone that I was no longer seeing the guy I had been dating for the last few years. She had met him on a trip he and I had taken to Florida once and she'd liked him. In fact, when I was in the bathroom and out of earshot, she'd told him that she'd like to have him for a grandson one day, a statement I could only blush and laugh at later when he relayed it back to me. She listened when I told her the relationship was over. She wasn't disappointed or upset, saying only, "You sound sad but not that sad." I smiled at that, finally knowing what it was I was feeling. She knew. She knew the messiness of heartbreak and disappointment, and their fleetingness too. Her words did not preach or apologize or prod; they only recognized. I'd felt something in that moment with her, something I had not felt before. It was the feeling of being seen and my, what an elusive feeling that can be.

I set my bag to the side and went to the kitchen to clean up the last of our dishes before leaving for the airport. The shuttle van would be here soon. I loaded Bubbie's dishwasher and looked for detergent under her sink. When I couldn't find any, I asked her what I should use. "Use the soap," she said. "That's fine."

I poured the blue liquid soap into the dishwasher and started the machine. Bubbie put on her sandals and I tied up my sneakers, ready for the cold weather back home. With my overfull duffel bag in hand, we walked toward the door, passing the kitchen on our way out. Bubbles were cascading down the dishwasher, along the front and onto the floor. Globs and globs of bubbles. "It's OK," she said, unbothered. How is that OK, I wondered, bubbles coating the floor and cabinets, making every surface slick. I had to laugh. I hadn't known the soap was going to create such a mess, and I couldn't tell whether or not she had. Though, to be fair, it remains the cleanest mess I've ever made.

We rode the elevator down to the lobby and headed outside. She had left her cane behind again and grabbed the crook of my arm for stability. Like that, I became her makeshift walker, tensing my muscles for support. We made our way to a bench in front of her building and waited for the shuttle van to come pick me up.

The air outside was thick, but the breeze that ran through it was a gentle whisper, straight from the ocean itself. The palm trees swayed, the string lights around their trunks still faintly glowing from being left on from the night before. Bubbie held my hand in hers as we sat on the bench. We had spent so much straight, uninterrupted time together that we didn't have much to say. Sometimes you do that, you run out of words to say. Sometimes you don't need any in the first place. Quiet can contain more than silence, more than shame; it has the capacity for closeness, too. She stroked my hand with hers, back and forth, as if it was me who was made out of a fleece-like fabric. I sat beside her, observing the calm and absorbing her touch. It was so easy for me to get caught up in the things Bubbie couldn't say or do that I missed what she did with ease. The way she loved me. The way she looked out. I didn't need an old diary or letters to tell her story. I had Bubbie herself and years of her love, forever building me up, pushing me in the right direction. She had offered me everything: her stories, her attention, her food, her time, her care. Her life may have been shaped by chaos, but it was this torrent of love that had shaped and surrounded mine.

When I first flew to Florida, I'd had no idea what I was getting myself into. Bubbie was never able to voice the stakes of our project, and I certainly did not know, either. Only sitting outside her building, my hand folded in hers, did I start to get it. She was in pain. She had been for years. She was asking me to help, to lift a little bit of it, to be a set of ears for her, another pair of hands. For the first time I was able to see this side of her, buried and bruised. She had been robbed of her humanity early in life and told it wasn't so. Later she tried to stuff it down when it became inconvenient, push it to the side when the sting grew too great. She made phone call after phone call asking me to write her story, and it took me a long time to see, but what she was asking for was more than a record of what happened. She wanted to be heard. She wanted to be seen, for someone to sit still and listen, to know her and her pain. My questions had not hurt her. They'd lightened her step.

Though I never had the words to express it, I also wanted this kind of closeness. I craved connection with

Bubbie and found it hard to come by. Our conversations were always so clumsy. I couldn't understand why nothing was ever easygoing with her. Only in Florida did I discover the value of the hardgoing, the challenging and complicated, the distressing and true. It ran us down and emptied us out. But also: it brought us together. The love we felt was not new, but the connection, the sense of closeness, was.

After a few minutes, the shuttle van pulled up to the building. I must've been the second pickup that day because a man in a business suit was already in the back, typing furiously on his phone. Bubbie gave me a hug and watched as I stepped into the van, setting my plumped-up duffel bag at my feet. She watched the shuttle drive down the street and didn't go back inside her building until it was well out of sight. I know because I was watching, too.

In the weeks after my trip, I would listen to our interviews over and over, transcribing every word. I'd spend a year deciphering the name Christianstadt alone. I was fixated on getting her story right. I wanted every detail. I wanted to look them in the face, to pull them out from the murk of the unknown. I had never paid much attention to my family's history before, never found it particularly interesting or important, but after Florida, I couldn't rest. I emailed museum curators and research specialists, ran searches through the Arolsen Archives and Yad Vashem, and amassed more documents on my relatives than any of us ever knew existed. So much had been deliberately destroyed in the war that we all assumed nothing was left. Perhaps rightly so. Some of the papers I found had been scanned into databases as recently as 2012. It was not happenstance that it took my family seventy-plus years to set the facts to paper.

Being part of the third generation is not an experience of survival, but of the echoes of survival. An echo that sounds like living, like forgetting, like still somehow knowing. For me, the experience was a thin film over the rest of my life. Not central, not current, not pressing, but there. I felt separate from what happened to my grandma. That separateness, that distance to the relative across the table, in the kitchen, at the salon, holding a cane but not using it, that's the third-generation experience. The loss appeared so far removed, it didn't feel like loss anymore. It felt like an ocean, too wide to cross.

At one point in my writing, my aunt would send me an email, saying, "I am so glad that Mom is talking to you, the bond between her and I could not handle the conversation. We are too close." For Bubbie and me, it was distance that made this work possible. We needed distance to see, and distance to share. It's what gave me the courage to push forward, to look where no one else in my family had been able to look. It was a gift, after all.

I would write before work and after, desperate to make the story whole. Every detail would unearth more questions, more chasms and cracks in the story. My writing was no longer for Bubbie alone, but for myself too. I'd find power in knowing what happened to my family, where I came from, what might be stashed away in my epigenetics. In her essay "Writing Advice for My Younger Self," poet and writer E.J. Koh says, "To research is to rehabilitate . . . words cannot only heal previous generations, they can reverse the trajectory of damage into future generations."[25] In those words, I would discover what it was I was doing, why I had become so obsessed. I was rehabilitating a broken story, mending an old familial wound. I'd been to physical therapy enough times as a climber to know the process: strengthen that which is weak, stretch that which is tight. Writing my grandma's story allowed me to strengthen my sense of the past and stretch my view of myself. I was not so disconnected, not so incapable. None of us are. For once, I could grasp Bubbie in all her forms: alone, terrified, cheerful, resilient. She was the boat that had all its boards changed out; she was the exact same. It no longer struck me as odd that my photo appeared at the end of her Shoah Foundation interview. It was a photo that brought her joy, that made her proud, a flourishing of family when there was so little family to flourish. And that was part of the narrative, too.

With every sentence I wrote, I would become more understanding. With every paragraph, more patient. The past would no longer seem so far away. I saw parallels in the news, the rise of nationalism, Nazis on social media, state-sponsored violence, kids in cages. I was sad in a way that was new to me; I was focused and angry and determined. The opposite of flattening a story is breathing air into it, inflating it to its full size and shape, and screaming when it becomes bigger than you.

As I'd write, my role in my family would shift. Questions Bubbie normally would've been asked started coming to me. When a distant relative sent around a photo with people she could not name, my family sent it my way and I named each and every person, knowing roughly where and when it'd been taken. I had never seen the picture before, none of us had, and we were stunned by its sudden appearance, its existence at all. It was a pre-war photo of Bubbie's immediate family. There she was, Goldie as a kid, as I'd never seen her before, age eight, her arm hooked around the arm of her grandma Malka. There were her brothers Mechel and Bumme, standing tall in the back row, their bodies framing a photo of their late father that'd been taped to the dropcloth behind them as if he too was present and posing. There was Blimchu wearing a polka dot dress, a sweet smile on her young face. There were the little ones, Meilekh and Rojha Blima, with docile eyes and full cheeks, and there was Henia, thin with grief, leaning toward the rest, her body angled like a shield. To my own surprise, I had become someone with a memory, someone with knowledge and names and detail. I had the capacity to hold it in my hands, this delicate information, to reckon with what was known and cope with what was not.

This wasn't just Bubbie's family. It was mine. How long it took me to have that thought.

Bubbie would give one more filmed interview after ours. Her memory was starting to fade and she invited me to join her, hoping I'd be able to fill in what she might leave out. We drove to the local Holocaust museum and a liaison led us to a large meeting room above the exhibit floor. A man clipped a microphone to my shirt and held another above Bubbie's head. We sat at the conference table, the camera directly across from us. As the interviewer posed his questions, Bubbie answered and I listened, adding to what she said or making slight (or not-so-slight) corrections. We fielded question after question like this. I was no longer a photo at the very end, but a presence in the room. To me, it felt like one of our reading sessions back at my parents' dining room table: Bubbie and I sitting side by side, our chairs unusually close, trying to make sense of all that around us.

In the coming years, both Bubbie and I would move to the Chicago area. I would get a job offer with a larger ad agency and she would get too old to be so far from family. For the first time since I was three, we'd live in the same state, only a few miles away. We'd spend more time together than we ever had before, walking laps in the warm-water pool at her senior living center, baking challah in her new, accessible apartment. We'd go to bingo together and she'd boast to anyone and everyone, "This is my granddaughter!" As I reached gaps in my writing, I would return to her apartment, asking her questions about moments from throughout her life. She'd answer openly, pleased someone wanted to know, and watch as I wrote her answers in my notebook. Eventually, I'd read her a full draft of the book out loud. "That's a good one," she said after I read a chapter containing nothing but her own words.

Remembrance can take as much as it can give. It can take the ignorance of youth, the narrowness of the present, the crisp blue color straight from the sky. When the weight of the work grew too great, I'd try to do as Bubbie did, digging into my love to make everything small again. We'd talk on the phone. We'd eat breakfast and sit in the sun. Her new building had a courtyard with flowering trees and lush green shrubs. We'd play Rummikub there, balancing the tiles on cooking mats so they wouldn't fall through the grates in the table. We'd watch *Shark Tank* and *American Ninja Warrior*. I'd print family photos for her to flip through. That's me, she'd say when she saw herself. That's my family. Was this how it's done? A language invented, a story like a ball of dough. We'd forge a new way to connect, a path that stretched beyond words. Not all forms of understanding require us to understand.

At certain moments I'd laugh, thinking about how she tricked me into becoming a better writer. Before my trip to Florida, my writing was mostly for work, client projects and campaign briefs. Now I lived inside my own documents, drafting, revising, editing, expanding. The voice, clear and curious, was mine. It was as simple as she'd said and also much, much harder.

In the shuttle van, my knee jumped up and down as south Florida rolled by outside. I stared out the window and watched as we drove past the hair salon and grocery store, the strip mall and gas station. The palm trees grew smaller, the billboards slipped in and out of view. Florida had sapped me as much as it filled me. I pulled my duffel bag onto my lap and turned to the window, my eyes fixed on the traffic and the green of the trees. I couldn't wait to take a nap on the plane. My head felt as stuffed as my bag. I hiccupped.

For many years, Bubbie believed that when a person had the hiccups, it meant someone was thinking about them. That was the reason behind their sudden spasming for air. Whenever she got a bout of the hiccups, she tried to figure out who was talking about her. That was the cure. "Must be Hedi," she'd say as she hiccupped after breakfast. "I think Harry's talking about me," she'd blurt between gulps of an afternoon snack. With both hands in the sink, scrubbing dirty dinner plates, she'd hiccup and tell me, "Your mom is talking about me again." I didn't believe as Bubbie did in this magical connection between other people's thoughts and one's own rapid intaking of air. It didn't make logical sense to me—or any sense for that matter. And yet, on the shuttle ride back to the airport, on the ramp headed toward Departures, I got the hiccups out of nowhere and could think of no one else but Golda Indig, shuffling about her condo, refusing to use her cane, thinking of me.

RECIPES

GOLDA INDIG'S POTATO LATKES

Notes: All quantities listed below can be described as close-ish estimates made by my mom and me. You think my grandma is measuring anything? If you really want to cook like her, ignore all my directions and watch the batter instead. If it's dry, add more liquid. If it's runny, add oatmeal. That's the secret. Cook something ten thousand times and you might get it right.

Ingredients:
5 potatoes, peeled
1 large onion
4 eggs
2½ tbsp. oatmeal (or ½ tbsp. per potato)
1 tsp. salt
¼ tsp. pepper
⅓ tsp. cup oil

Directions:

1. Grate the potatoes and onion into a large bowl. Try not to knick your finger.

2. Add in the eggs, oatmeal, salt, and pepper, and stir.

3. Heat the oil in a pan on the stove. When the oil is hot, form the mixture into thin round patties and cook until crispy, flipping halfway through with a fork.

4. When latkes are golden brown, move them to a plate with a paper towel. Blot off the grease before serving, then, serve, serve, serve, serve, serve.

GOLDA INDIG'S CREAMISH

Notes: If you make this for your neighbors, they might give you a funny look like, What is this thing? But the next day, they'll come over raving, their lips still touched with powdered sugar and cream. All right, no, they will have washed their faces by then, but you'll imagine them like that, all messy and enchanted, their eyes aglow, and it will make you happy. If desserts aren't about happiness, what are they?

Ingredients – Pastry Dough:
4 cups flour
1 lb. butter, softened
4 egg yolks
16 oz. sour cream (or cream cheese)

Ingredients – Custard Filling:
3 vanilla pudding mixes (3 oz. each)
6 cups whole milk
2 tbsp. cornstarch
1 tsp. vanilla extract

Directions:
1. To make the dough, knead flour and softened butter together. Gradually add the egg yolks and

sour cream. Add more flour if the dough becomes too sticky. Roll the dough into a ball, cover and refrigerate overnight.

2. Coat a saucepan with butter. Add 4 cups of milk and bring to a simmer.

3. Mix 1½ cups of cold milk with pudding mixes, then add to the heated milk.

4. In a separate bowl, mix ½ cup of milk with the cornstarch and add to the mixture.

5. When a few bubbles appear in the milk mixture, add in vanilla extract and remove the pan from the stove.

6. Cover the saucepan with cling film and refrigerate overnight.

7. Take the dough out of the fridge and let soften.

8. Preheat oven to 400 degrees Fahrenheit. Place parchment paper on two cookie sheets.

9. Cut the ball of dough in half. Roll it out to the size of a cookie sheet and place it on top of the parchment paper. Do this twice.

10. Dock the sheets of dough using a fork. Be thorough; there should be small holes every inch or so.

11. Cook the dough for 5-10 minutes. Remove from the oven when the pastry is a light golden color. Let cool completely.

12. Scoop pudding filling onto one of the pastry sheets. Make even. Slide the second pastry sheet over top.

13. Sprinkle powdered sugar generously. A little more. A little more, still. More. Refrigerate until ready to serve.

GOLDA INDIG'S CRESCENT ROLL COOKIES

Notes: My grandma Golda learned to make crescent rolls when her grandma Malka first showed her how. They're a nutty delight of a cookie, equal parts buttery, flaky and sweet. The only downside of the crescent roll is that it's not so great in the mail, a fact I know because my grandma used to send me a batch every other month while I was in college. She packed the cookies in empty shoeboxes, adding chocolate bars and paper towels for padding. Then, she'd wrap the whole thing in brown paper and let USPS do their thing. Crumbs. Instantly and everywhere. Luckily, even when battered and broken, my grandma's crescent roll cookies are delicious.

Ingredients - Dough:
4 cups flour
1 lb. butter, softened
4 egg yolks
16 oz. sour cream (or cream cheese)

Ingredients - Filling:
1 package walnuts, chopped (10 oz.)
1 cup sugar
4 egg whites

Directions:

1. Mix the flour, butter, yolks and sour cream to form a dough. Leave overnight in the refrigerator.

2. In a bowl, combine walnuts, sugar and eggs whites to make the filling for the cookies.

3. Sprinkle flour onto a clean surface. Roll the dough into a thin sheet then cut it into triangles, about three or four inches long.

4. Spoon the walnut filling onto the base of each triangle. Roll the dough to cover the filling. Keep going until the whole cookie is rolled up.

5. Bake at 400 degrees Fahrenheit, seam side down, for 15 minutes or until the crescent rolls have a light golden brown color and are impossible to resist. Eat immediately or freeze for later.

PHOTOS

Golda stands with her family in a photo studio. The photo, circa 1937 or 1938, survived the war solely because it was sent to an aunt in the United States. It is the only known pre-war photo of Golda and her siblings. From left to right, top row: Henia, Blimchu, Mechel, a still photograph of Peretz, and Bumme Feuerwerger. Bottom row: Rojha Blima, Malka, Golda and Meilekh Feuerwerger.

Golda, age 17, and Benti, age 25, on their wedding day.
Golda wears a borrowed dress.

```
Date    12.5.5o/Ho G                    Kunig L.
Name  I N D I G    Golda          Fil 6-1222/BR
BD 19 y.        BP Roumania       Nat Roum.-Jew
Next of Kin
Source of Information Intern.Mov.Office Bremen-Grohn
Last kn. Location Bremerhaven        Date
CC/Prison             Arr.              lib.
Transkxx 12.4.5o emigr.to Canada on MSTS"Gen.
Died on                 in               MCRae"
Cause of death
Buried on               in
Grave                         D.C.No.
Remarks                     l. A. i 26
```

Golda's emigration card documents her departure from Germany on April 12, 1950. She was 19 years old when she boarded the MSTS General McRae to Canada. I can't help but notice the blank "Next of Kin" line.

Outside their home in Windsor, Canada, in the summer of 1959, Golda and her kids stand like dominos. From left to right: Gail, Harry, Hedi, and Golda Indig.

An avid cook, Golda makes cookies with me, her youngest grandchild, in my family's old home in Michigan.

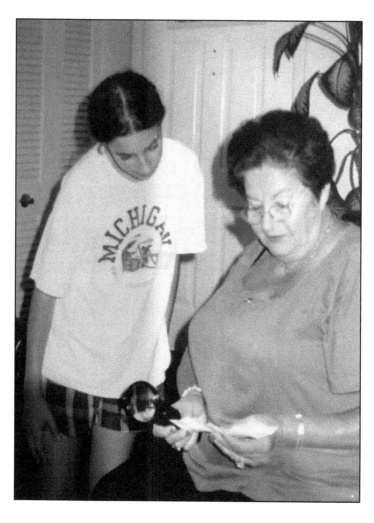

During one of our reading lessons together, Golda holds a magnifying glass and a piece of paper with a sentence I wrote for her. I'm wearing my favorite shorts, blue and yellow pajama pants that she hemmed into shorts for me.

In the midst of working on this book, Golda and I take a break to enjoy ourselves at a family event. My brother Scott, who took this photo, shouts, "Give her a kiss!" And Golda does.

FOOTNOTES

1 Ruth Franklin, A Thousand Darknesses: Lies and Truth in Holocaust Fiction (Oxford University Press, 2010).

2 "Wannsee Conference and the 'Final Solution,'" United States Holocaust Memorial Museum (United States Holocaust Memorial Museum), https://encyclopedia.ushmm.org/content/en/article/wannsee-conference-and-the-final-solution.

3 "'It Started With Words' – Holocaust Survivors Give Stunning Testimonies to Mark Holocaust Remembrance Day," #ItStartedWithWords, April 8, 2021, https://itstartedwithwords.org/about/.

4 Randall Bytwerk, "Caricatures from Der Stürmer: 1933-1945," German Propaganda Archive, 1998, https://research.calvin.edu/german-propaganda-archive/sturmer.htm.

5 "Spelling of antisemitism," International Holocaust Remembrance Alliance, April 2015, http://holocaustremembrance.com/resources/spelling-antisemitism.

6 "Working definition of antisemitism," International Holocaust Remembrance Alliance, May 2016, https://holocaustremembrance.com/resources/working-definition-antisemitism/.

7 "Human Rights and other Civil Society Groups Urge United Nations to Respect Human Rights in the Fight Against Antisemitism." Human Rights Watch, April 2023, https://www.hrw.org/news/2023/04/04/human-rights-and-other-civil-society-groups-urge-united-nations-respect-human.

8 "Auschwitz," United States Holocaust Memorial Museum, https://encyclopedia.ushmm.org/content/en/article/auschwitz.

9 Amy J. Sindler , Nancy S. Wellman, and Oren Baruch Stier, "Holocaust Survivors Report Long-Term Effects on Attitudes toward Food," Journal of Nutrition Education and Behavior 36, 4. (July 2004): 189-196. https://www.jneb.org/article/S1499-4046(06)60233-9/pdf.

10 Rachel Yehuda, Linda M. Bierer, Ruth Andrew, James Schmeidler, and Jonathan R. Seckl. "Enduring Effects Of Severe Developmental Adversity, Including Nutritional Deprivation, On Cortisol Metabolism In Aging Holocaust Survivors." Journal Of Psychiatric Research 43, 9 (June 2009): 877-883. https://www.sciencedirect.com/science/article/abs/pii/S0022395608002689

11 Tori Rodriguez. "Descendants Of Holocaust Survivors Have Altered Stress Hormones". Scientific American 26 (2). https://www.scientificamerican.com/article/descendants-of-holocaust-survivors-have-altered-stress-hormones/

12 Naama Fund, Ash Nachman, Avi Porath, Varda Shalev, Gideon Koren. "Comparison of Mortality and Comorbidity Rates Between Holocaust Survivors and Individuals in the General Population in Israel." JAMA Network Open. (2019). https://jamanetwork.com/journals/jamanetworkopen/fullarticle/2720067

13 Daniel Blatman, *The Death Marches: The Final Phase of Nazi Genocide* (Belknap Press of Harvard University Press, 2011)

14 Ruth Kluger, *Still Alive: A Holocaust Girlhood Remembered* (Feminist Press, 2001).

[15] "British Army Chaplain Describes Bergen-Belsen Upon Liberation," United States Holocaust Memorial Museum. https://encyclopedia.ushmm.org/content/en/film/british-army-chaplain-describes-bergen-belsen-upon-liberation.

[16] Bernice Lerner, *All the Horrors of War: A Jewish Girl, a British Doctor, and the Liberation of Bergen-Belsen* (Johns Hopkins University Press, 2020).

[17] "Murder of Hungarian Jewry," Yad Vashem. https://www.yadvashem.org/holocaust/about/fate-of-jews/hungary.html.

[18] "New study reveals biological toll on brain function of Holocaust survivors." Spink Health, 2019. https://www.eurekalert.org/pub_releases/2019-06/sh-nsr062419.php

[19] Abraham Sagi-Schwartz, Marinus H. van IJzendoorn, Klaus E. Grossmann, Tirtsa Joels, Karin Grossmann, Miri Scharf, Nina Koren-Karie, and Sarit Alkalay. "Attachment and Traumatic Stress in Female Holocaust Child Survivors and Their Daughters." *American Journal of Psychiatry* 160, 6 (June 2003): 1086-1092. https://ajp.psychiatryonline.org/doi/pdf/10.1176/appi.ajp.160.6.1086

[20] Hédi Fried, *Questions I Am Asked about the Holocaust*, trans. Alice E. Olsson. Scribe, 2019.

[21] Ingrid Rojas Contreras, *The Man Who Could Move Clouds: A Memoir*. New York: Anchor, 2023.

[22] Viet Thanh Nguyen, *Nothing Ever Dies: Vietnam and the Memory of War*. Harvard University Press, 2017.

[23] Rebecca Clifford, *Survivors: Children's Lives after the Holocaust* (Yale University Press, 2020).

[24] S.Y. Gross and Y. Yosef Cohen, eds., *The Marmaros Book* (Tel Aviv: Beit Marmaros, 1983).

[25] E.J. Koh, "Writing Advice for My Younger Self," Catapult, March 4, 2020, https://catapult.co/stories/essay-writing-advice-for-my-younger-self-ej-koh.

ACKNOWLEDGEMENTS

Writing this book took nine years, from my late twenties to my mid-thirties. To the relatives and family friends who shared their memories with me, especially the painful ones, the ones we've all worked so hard to forget, thank you.

To my early readers, including the Frontyard Writers Group in Philadelphia, thank you for your encouragement and insight. Thanks especially to Chris Santantasio and Nicole White for reading multiple early drafts. Thanks to Katie Adams, Lilly Dancyger, Helen Betya Rubinstein, Jill Swenson, and Anca L. Szilágyi for seeing things I could not, and to Megan Stielstra for teaching me to attack my bookshelves. Thank you to my friend and former co-editor at *Chestnut Review* Nadia Staikos for her wisdom, laughter and commiseration.

Many, many thanks to Jerry Brennan at Tortoise Books for his belief in this book, and to Caitlin Hamilton Summie for her support on all things promotion. Thanks to Ali Doucette for giving this book such a striking cover.

Thank you to the friends who kept my spirits up, even (and maybe especially) when they didn't know they were down. Being there without being asked is an amazing gift to give someone. I'm grateful to my parents Derek & Gail Randel, who do this every day. They've listened, read and supported me endlessly. Thanks to my brother Scott Randel, a machine of encouragement. He hyped this project to friends and told me I was doing a great job despite having no idea what I was doing. I am supremely lucky to be his sister. Thanks also to Dana, Abe and Theo Randel for being themselves.

Thank you to my husband and love, Aaron Meyer.

This book would not exist if my grandma had not pushed me into it. Thank you, Bubbie. What a mark you've left on the world and what a mark you've left on me. No, I'm not hungry right now. Maybe later. I love you.

ABOUT THE AUTHOR

Brooke Randel is a writer, editor, and associate creative director in Chicago. Her writing has been published in *Hippocampus*, *Hypertext Magazine*, *Jewish Fiction*, *SmokeLong Quarterly*, and elsewhere. The granddaughter of a Holocaust survivor, she writes on issues of memory, trauma, family and history. Find more of her work at www.brookerandel.com.

ABOUT TORTOISE BOOKS

Slow and steady wins in the end, even in publishing. Tortoise Books is dedicated to finding and promoting quality authors who haven't yet found a niche in the marketplace—writers producing memorable and engaging works that will stand the test of time.

Learn more at www.tortoisebooks.com or follow us on Twitter (assuming the website still exists when you're reading this) @TortoiseBooks.